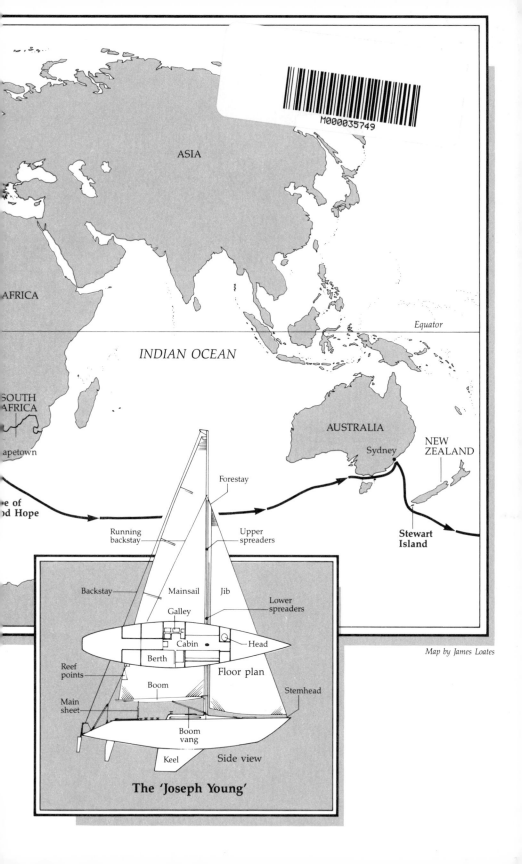

ASIA

AFRICA

Equator

INDIAN OCEAN

SOUTH
AFRICA

apetown

AUSTRALIA

Sydney

NEW
ZEALAND

e of
d Hope

Forestay

Running
backstay

Upper
spreaders

**Stewart
Island**

Map by James Loates

Backstay

Mainsail   Jib

Galley

Lower
spreaders

Cabin

Head

Berth

Floor plan

Reef
points

Boom

Main
sheet

Boom
vang

Stemhead

Keel   Side view

The 'Joseph Young'

THE SAILING SPIRIT

Meeting the BOC Challenge

THE SAILING SPIRIT

John Hughes

SEAL BOOKS
McClelland-Bantam Inc.
Toronto

THE SAILING SPIRIT
A Seal Book / December 1988

Canadian Cataloguing in Publication Data

Hughes, John (John G.)
Sailing spirit

ISBN 0-7704-2280-2

1. Hughes, John (John G.).   2. BOC Challenge Race.
3. Yacht racing.   I. Title.

GV832.H83 1988   797.1′4′0924   C88-094717-9

PRINTED IN CANADA

0 9 8 7 6 5 4 3 2 1

Contents

Prologue

May 27, 1987. 1644 hours local time. The sound of the finishing gun rolled across the oily, calm waters off Newport, Rhode Island. Alone aboard my yacht *Joseph Young*, a feeling of unmatched satisfaction washing over me, I raised my arms in a brief moment of triumph. All that long day we had been creeping forward under a blazing hot sun, occasional puffs of wind stirring the sails, moving us agonizingly closer to the land. Now, at last, after 225 days and 28,553 nautical miles, the circle was closed; *Joseph Young* and I had completed our solo circumnavigation of the world.

As the sound of the gun faded, pandemonium broke out all around me. The small fleet of spectator boats that had come to welcome me home gave a rousing salute: whistles were blowing, there was waving and cheering, and flares and water cannon were fired off. I was filled with a sense of pride. It seemed strange, after so long alone on the open sea, to be the centre of such attention. Up on the foredeck, dropping the sails for the last time, I looked back over the small yacht that had seen me safely through some rough times. She showed few scars indeed —a scratch here, a bent stanchion there—but for me, each was a glaring reminder of some incident in the hard voyage now finally at an end. This was not the time for reflection, however; the Race Committee boat was approaching rapidly across the water and would soon be alongside. Hurriedly stowing the sail,

1

I clambered back to the cockpit just as it pulled up gently beside *Joseph Young*. Aboard were my mother, brother, my girlfriend, Vicki, and several close friends. With the exception of Vicki, I had not seen any of my family since I had left Newport some nine months before. It had been a long and lonely race around the world.

I had set out from Newport in August of 1986 as one of the competitors in the second running of what has been called the marathon of all yacht races. Officially organized and sponsored by the British Oxygen Company (now the BOC Group Ltd.), the event is known as the BOC Challenge. All entrants in the race were to sail, alone, from Newport, Rhode Island, west to east around the world, by way of the Cape of Good Hope, Australia, and Cape Horn.

For me, entering the BOC Challenge was not so much a decision as it was the culmination of a boyhood dream of a life of adventure at sea. As a child growing up in England, I had spent every holiday with my grandparents on the south coast of Cornwall, where "messing about in boats" was a favourite pastime. Hours spent bobbing around in our family's small sailing dinghy taught me the rudimentary skills, and whetted my appetite for things nautical. Reading books by Sir Francis Chichester, Robin Knox-Johnston, Chay Blyth, and others, had instilled in me a sense of curiosity about what it was like out there over the horizon. By the time I was thirteen, a year before we moved to Canada, notions of being a farmer or fireman had long been dispelled; a career in the Merchant Navy was all that bore thinking about.

My family's move to Thunder Bay, Ontario, did nothing to quell my urge to go to sea. Using the money saved from my after-school job as sexton of a downtown church, I purchased a set of building plans for a fifteen-foot sailboat. Over the course of the ensuing winter, all my time, energy, and savings went into the construction of "The Boat," built from scratch, save for the purchased suit of sails. I was never so proud as on the day she was launched for the first time. During my last summer at

2

home, my every spare moment was spent sailing up and down the confines of the harbour, dreaming always of the open ocean.

In my last year in high school I decided to go on to a three-year marine navigation program at Georgian College in southern Ontario. The course, half of which involved practical training as a cadet aboard ship, was designed to provide navigation officers for Canadian merchant ships. Thus, four weeks after graduating from high school, prepared only by a brief ten-day orientation period at college, I found myself reporting aboard my first ship. Three years later I graduated with the qualifications needed for employment as a Second Officer in the Merchant Navy, sharing the responsibility for the safe navigation of the ship. I embarked on my career at sea.

The next few years at sea were good ones. Working on ships trading from the Baltic to the China Sea, from the African coast to the high Arctic, in the Mediterranean and Caribbean seas, and around the coasts of Europe provided an interesting way of life, and satisfied my urge to be on the ocean. My time off work was spent studying to improve my qualifications. I was far from bored, but something was missing. Bigger ships and high technology had, it seemed, distanced the professional seaman from the sea. Somehow, the satisfaction that can come only from a real challenge eluded me.

Home on leave in the fall of 1981 I came across a short article in a sailing magazine concerning a single-handed around-the-world race, scheduled to start on August 2, 1982. The race would start and finish in Newport, Rhode Island, and was to be sponsored by the British Oxygen Company. I was captivated. Such a race provided a reason, within an organized framework, for doing something basically nonsensical—sailing solo around the world. Unfortunately, a lack of both time and money, and my desire to obtain a Master Mariner's or Captain's Certificate as soon as possible precluded my even contemplating actually entering the race. I did, however, follow very closely the progress of the competitors as they made their way around the course over the next year and a half.

3

Nineteen-eighty-four found me living in Halifax. My career in the Merchant Navy had led me to a position as Chief Mate (and eventually Captain) aboard one of the offshore supply tugs being operated by Husky Oil. Working at sea on a month-on month-off schedule, our job was to tow, tend, and supply the oil rigs engaged in exploration off the east coast of Canada. I had just completed my Master Mariner's Certificate and my months off were no longer taken up with studying. Although the work at sea was both interesting and enjoyable, the months off seemed aimless. Boredom set in; I no longer had goals to aim for in the foreseeable future. A steady job, good income, lots of free time on leave, all stretched out ahead as a rather dull existence.

I was lingering over coffee one morning, browsing through yet another sailing magazine and counting the few days left at home before returning to sea, when a one-paragraph article sprang into focus. As I read, a warm flush of excitement spread over me. British Oxygen Company, it was announced, had decided to sponsor a second around-the-world single-handed yacht race. To be known as the BOC Challenge, the race was scheduled to start on August 30, 1986. An address was given, and prospective competitors were invited to write in for a set of the race rules and an information package. My mind, as I laid down the magazine, was in a whirl. Was this, perhaps, the challenge that I sought? I composed myself while finishing my coffee, then took out pen and paper and sat down at the desk. Writing away for a set of the race rules was, I told myself, merely an exercise in curiosity. It was obviously out of the question for me to actually enter the race; I had no offshore sailing experience, I had no boat, the sponsorship required to design and build a competitive entry would be next to impossible to come by, and, quite frankly, the whole idea really scared the hell out of me! Still, it would be interesting to find out what the race requirements were. Enclosing my five dollars for the information package and return postage, I sealed the envelope.

When I returned home on leave a month later I wasted no time before sorting through the bundle of mail waiting for me.

Excitedly I pulled out a large envelope from the BOC Race Head-quarters. Opening it, I felt as if I was dipping my toe into deep water, not sure whether to take the plunge. The rules themselves were fairly simple; the race was to be divided into two classes, Class Two for boats between forty and fifty feet in length, and Class One for boats between fifty and sixty feet in length. The speed of a boat being primarily dependent on its length, it was obvious that one would need a fifty-footer to win Class Two, or a sixty-footer to win Class One. The race was to start on August 30, 1986, and in order to qualify one had to complete a 2,000-mile solo ocean crossing in the boat to be sailed in the race.

For the next week or two I read and reread the information from the race organizers, took long walks, and did some serious soul-searching. I knew that entering the BOC Challenge would be an enormous undertaking, one that I was not sure, in my heart, I was ready for. Rationalizing, I decided that I would start looking for a corporate backer for a Class-One boat without actually committing myself in any way. There would be no risk to me whatsoever. This gave me a nice easy buffer against actually taking the plunge, and it occupied my leaves for the next ten months. Trips to the library yielded the names of corporations and their executives to whom I wrote innumerable letters outlining my proposal for entering a Canadian yacht in the upcoming BOC Challenge. Without exception they wrote back. Without exception, they expressed their regrets that it did not tie in with their ideas on public relations, wishing me, however, every success in my future endeavours. By late summer it had become evident that corporate sponsorship was not to be had. A crossroads had been reached. I had to ask myself, and decide for myself, if the BOC Challenge was, in fact, something that I really wanted. At this point, it would have been easy for me to decide to forget the whole idea. Nobody was aware of my interest in the race so there was no outside pressure on me to pursue the idea. For my own peace of mind, I had a legitimate excuse: sponsorship was unavailable. To go now, on my own resources, would be to go in the smallest allowable boat, precluding any chance of actually winning the race. My decision was, in fact, simplified. Did I or didn't I want to realize my dream of sailing alone around the world? There probably would never be another time in my life when circumstances would allow me the choice. I felt lucky; few people ever find themselves able to chase a dream. I decided that, for me, entering the race and finishing was the most important thing; winning was not. I was prepared to give it my all simply to count myself among the competitors. With this hurdle crossed, the search began for a suitable boat in the (affordable, I hoped) forty-foot range.

I found her some four months later at the Dockside Boat Show in Toronto. It was, at the risk of appearing sentimental, love at first sight. Having examined hundreds of stock designs by this time, I had more than a fair idea of what was available and I was starting to despair about ever finding a production hull that I could feel confident with. Off-the-shelf sailboats seemed to fall into three categories. First, there were the heavy cruising yachts, built as if to withstand nuclear attack and able to carry enough supplies to sustain you and yours for months at sea (which is about how long you would need to sail these boats from Halifax to Chester if the wind was against you). Second, there were the round-the-buoys racers, with rule-beating lumps and bumps that gave the look of a bottlenose dolphin with thyroid problems, and requiring a full crew on deck to keep everything under control. And third, there was the hybrid racer/ cruiser that promised the whole family luxury accommodation within the confines of a forty-foot Tupperware box akin to a motorhome with sails.

The Cayenne 41 was none of the above. She looked ''right,'' and had, in stock form, most of the features for racing around the world that I was looking for. Designed by Swedish naval architect Hakan Sodegren and built in Sweden by Comfortbätar AB, she proved to be everything hoped for — and more. Although having the boat built ''out of sight'' was not my first choice, the enthusiasm shown by the builder for the project, the co-operation I received in making the necessary modifications, and the quality of the finished boat more than made up for the hassles associated with having it built overseas. After lengthy negotiations with the builder's Canadian representative, Sailtech Inc., a contract was signed. My boat would be delivered to me in Halifax in July of 1985. It was now January 1985. The race was due to start in nineteen months.

The Cayenne has a typically Swedish narrow hull, with a beam of only 8'9" on an overall length of 41'2". Built of modern materials (Kevlar, S-glass, and Divynicell), which are both lighter and stronger than regular fibreglass, the finished boat weighed in at just under 12,000 pounds fully rigged.

The BOC's construction rules called for several features to improve the ''survivability'' of the yacht. The most significant design change required was the installation of two watertight bulkheads dividing the hull into three separate compartments, the idea being that the boat would remain afloat with any one section flooded. Each watertight section could be pumped out from the cockpit via its own pump and piping system. In addition, the two aft cockpit lockers and the main cockpit locker were completely separate compartments. Further changes to the stock design to improve the integrity of the hull involved the elimination of the standard companionways to both the main and the aft cabins. Access to the main cabin was via a top sliding hatch, to the aft cabin (which served strictly as a large storage space), via one of two small hatches.

Further changes were made to the boat to reduce and redistribute weight with an eye towards improving performance and the motion of the boat. The single water tank normally located under the starboard quarterberth was eliminated and replaced with two forty-gallon tanks, placed directly to port and starboard of the keel, as low in the boat as possible. Made of stainless steel, these tanks were bonded to the hull and bolted to fore and aft supports. Each tank had its own piping system and pump to prevent loss of the entire water supply in the event of damage to or contamination of one tank.

The builder quite ingeniously came up with another way of concentrating weight in the keel area; a watertight battery locker

7

was built into the aftermost portion of the bilge well. All four batteries were housed here, two deep, one behind the other. For charging the batteries a 9 hp Volvo diesel was installed, which proved more than powerful enough to turn the 70-amp alternator (a 50-amp unit being carried as a spare). No propeller shaft or transmission was installed aboard the boat, as the rules prohibited the use of mechanical propulsion.

Belowdecks, the living arrangements in the cabin were best described as functional. The galley, or kitchen, was on the port side as one entered through the main hatch, and boasted a small two-burner stove (no oven), a sink, several food lockers, and drawers for utensils. Opposite the galley, on the starboard side of the boat, was the chart table, navigational instruments, and the electrical panel. The head of the quarterberth served as a seat for the chart table, while the remainder of the berth extended aft under the floor of the cockpit. Forward of this there was a settee/berth on the starboard side and a long workbench on the port side, both built above the two fresh-water tanks. Right at the front of the cabin were the head, or toilet, and a hanging locker for clothes. The forward watertight bulkhead separated the cabin from the large sail locker, which occupied the remainder of the interior.

Financial constraints and a desire to keep things simple meant that no heating system, shower, or hot-water tank were installed. Entertainment was provided by a cassette player, music being something I could not bear the thought of doing without.

On deck, some modifications had to be made so that the boat would be easier for me to handle alone. Basically, this involved installing a number of extra winches so that control of the various lines required less time and effort. The two most important pieces of equipment that were added, however, were the self-steering gear and the auto-pilot. These would be my extra pair of hands during the course of the voyage, freeing me from the endless chore of steering the boat. Both items would keep the boat on course while I ate, slept, changed sails, or worked on other jobs. The self-steering gear, or windvane, was a large unit made of stainless steel, mounted on a frame attached to the stern of the boat. Through a system of gears and pulleys, it would maintain a constant heading relative to the wind direction. The auto-pilot, on the other hand, would keep the yacht on a set compass course, relying on an electrically driven control unit to turn the rudder.

All in all, the changes made to the boat proved successful. Undoubtedly, without financial constraints, further modifications to both the interior and the deck would have improved comfort and performance. In the final analysis, however, she carried me safely through some rough waters without letting me down, and for that I owe much to the men who built her.

The winter and spring of 1985, although busy, passed agonizingly slowly as I awaited the delivery of my boat to the Dartmouth Yacht Club. To scrape together enough money to purchase ancillary equipment for the boat I had to work some back-to-back shifts offshore and spend time on leave as a substitute driver on the Halifax harbour pilot boat. In between times, endless lists were compiled in preparation for the qualifying voyage to the United Kingdom, a trip I hoped to complete in the late summer or early fall.

It was during this period, as I tried to anticipate what preparations the yacht would actually require in order to make her truly seaworthy, that "the boat" took on a name. It was not a sudden inspiration, but rather a gradual process that led me to name the yacht after my late grandfather, Joseph Young. When I had first gone to sea at the age of sixteen, he and I had written letters back and forth on a regular basis. His interest in things nautical helped us share a special friendship that I will never forget. His death, which I learned of while standing in a dilapidated phone booth on the end of a coal dock, calling home during another hitch on board ship, was a great loss to me. Now, as I worked on preparations for this ultimate voyage, I knew how much he would have loved to have shared it with me. To name the yacht *Joseph Young* seemed natural.

Finally, in mid-July, a container ship steamed into Halifax

harbour, the *Joseph Young* part of her cargo. I was determined to cross the Atlantic before winter set in; waiting for spring would simply not leave enough time to plan and carry out any changes necessitated by the experience gained during the crossing. Working at a fever pitch for the latter part of July and the month of August, we got the boat sanded and painted, launched, rigged, and generally sorted out. David, my brother, devoted many long hours to the cause, and friends would occasionally drop by to lend a hand. The Very High Frequency (VHF) radio, used for short-range communications, and the Single-Sideband radio (SSB) with an optimal range of a few thousand miles, were installed, self-steering fitted, compass, lights, log, and anemometer hooked up and all systems tested. We even found time for a few trips around the harbour to check rigging and sails before I was called back to work in September. It would be early October before I returned home for my next leave. Time was now at a premium; fall gales were already creeping across the Eastern Seaboard. I hoped that my month back at sea with Husky Oil would not extend beyond the normal thirty days.

Fortunately, everything went according to schedule, and by the time the first of October rolled around I was back in Halifax. Knowing that I was determined to get on my way as soon as possible, friends rallied around to help load supplies of food and to take care of the myriad small items still not crossed off the last of my many lists. Finally, on the evening of October 5, I fell asleep knowing that tomorrow the adventure would begin.

October 6, 1985. *For the first time,* Joseph Young *and I are alone. The fear, apprehension, and anxiety which has peaked over the last six days is fading as rapidly as is the coast of Nova Scotia astern. Mere questions remain; will we be able to complete the qualifier in one piece? Will it meet my expectations and dreams? Maybe I'll hate it. What will it be like to be alone?*

Despite the nearly 2,700 miles of Atlantic Ocean that lay ahead of me before a landfall in England, I was more relaxed at that moment than I had been at any other time in the preceding six months. There was no longer any point in worrying about the thousand and one items that crop up when preparing for such a trip. What was done was done; what was not would remain so. I had finally taken a deep breath and plunged.

The first afternoon at sea was nearly perfect. With the moderate south-west wind *Joseph Young* was reaching comfortably towards the south-east with the #3 jib and one reef in the main sail. The self-steering was doing an excellent job and I was more than content to merely sit in the cockpit, enjoying the feeling of actually being under way. As the sun approached the horizon the wind eased a bit and I shook out the reef in the main, trimmed the sails, and took a last look around before slipping below to christen the coffee pot. Being slightly anxious about encounters with the east-coast fishing fleet, I didn't turn in at all that first night, sustaining myself with coffee in copious quantities and handfuls of dried fruit and chocolate. Except for a sail change at 0200, however, the night passed quietly, and shortly after sunrise I turned in for a few hours' sleep.

The next four days passed without incident, the barometer gently rising and falling, and the wind swinging from south to west and back again, blowing steadily between Force 5 and 6 on the Beaufort Scale. The weather was wet and cold with continual rain showers, but that was allright because we were also going fast. The log, or speedometer, hovered between 8 and 10 knots the whole time. I was really enjoying it. Each time the wind came round westerly and the barometer crept up I expected the sky to clear and the speed to tail off with the wind, but always the barometric pressure started down again and the wind veered back to the south.

I had finished a meal of baked beans and pilot biscuits and was firmly wedged between the quarterberth and the companionway steps, a mug of tea clasped tightly in both hands, enjoying the warmth it had to offer. On deck, the rain had turned to drizzle shortly after nightfall; although the wind was still Force 5 it was at least still westerly, and with any luck it might clear enough for a sun sight by morning. Not having been able to get a fix since leaving Halifax it would be nice to have even a single sextant shot of the sun with which to compare my dead-reckoning position. A bit of excitement had occurred earlier in the day when, sticking my head up on deck, I had found a fleet of Spanish trawlers less than a mile off to the south. Looking at the chart I realized I must be crossing the Tail of the Bank, a prime fishing ground, which put me a little to the north of the dead reckoning.

On the sixth day I woke suddenly with the sense of something not quite right. Going straight up on deck, I found that the shackle on the boom vang (a device for keeping downward tension on the boom) had parted. The wind had come round to the south-south-east and had dropped off to Force 2. The self-steering had faithfully followed the wind shift, and we were now heading north-north-east. After repairing the boom vang, I took down the #3 jib, set the #1 Genoa in its place, and shook the single reef out of the main. Sails trimmed, *Joseph Young* was set back on a course to the south-east. There was a heavy swell rolling in from the west and the barometer had fallen five millibars (a millibar being a unit used to measure pressure) in the last four hours. All the signs pointed to some nasty weather moving in from astern, not a bad time to make some miles to the south.

Within hours I had to abandon my south-easterly course and run off directly before the building wind and sea. The experience of surfing downwind on a forty-one-foot boat I can only describe as incredible! As the approaching sea rolled up from behind, *Joseph Young* would be picked up as if in an elevator. The whole boat would tilt downward until little rivulets of water were trickling back over the stemhead, and at times I was sure the bow was going to bury itself. Then, as we reached the crest of the swell, the wind hit us with full force as we were lifted out of the lee. After a second's hesitation the bow would lift and the whole boat would come alive. The sound would start as a low moan (caused, I think, by a slight vibration in the rudder) when the log reached 12 knots and build to a high-pitched scream as the log raced up over 23 knots. As the stern sank reluctantly back behind the crest of the overtaking wave, the scream would die away to a last wail of protest in anticipation of the next swell already climbing up behind us. The spray, too, was incredible, rising as a solid sheet from a point just forward of the mast on either side of the hull until it threatened to reach the lower spreaders on the mast, some twenty feet above the deck. At times, just for a second, I could see clear over the bow between these two curtains of water rising on either side of me, then they would be dashed back in my face, as if someone had turned a fire hose on me, forcing me to duck my head and close my eyes. I found myself laughing out loud with excitement.

Eighteen hours later I was no longer laughing. A problem with the windvane self-steering had kept me at the helm for the last fourteen hours and the cold and wet were taking their toll. My concentration was all but gone. I didn't actually see the wave that caught us, but I did hear it as it came roaring up at *Joseph Young* from the starboard quarter. As we started going over I fought to bring the bow to port, but it was already too late. When I found myself standing vertically on the side of the cockpit, I involuntarily let go of the tiller and, turning quickly, wrapped both arms around a winch and braced for what was to come. The wave broke. Underwater now, I was totally disoriented. It seemed ages before *Joseph Young* righted herself. The shock of the cold water had me wide awake now, and I grabbed for the tiller. As I steered my injured yacht downwind once more, we lifted soggily over the next swell. The waist-high water in the cockpit drained quickly away. Looking forward, I saw definite problems. The jib was badly torn and flogging widly. Worse yet, the boom was hanging like a broken wing, sheared almost in two by the force of the water. My spirits sank and I cursed my stupidity for not reducing sail sooner.

Fear now the motivation, I picked the right moment between swells and quickly turned the boat around until she was heading into the wind. On my hands and knees, I crawled forward to haul down what was left of the jib and stow it below. Moving back to the mast I dropped the main, winched the boom inboard, and securely lashed the whole works. I groped my way aft, exhausted and somewhat surprised at how well the boat was behaving with the tiller lashed down to leeward. As I slumped in the cockpit, I was, at that moment, very close to quitting. It took a lot of goading by my alter ego to get me moving again. "Fix the self-steering; see how she runs under bare poles." Surprise — 7 sometimes 8 knots, and steering herself. Thankfully, I dragged myself down below and brewed a mug of cocoa. Twenty minutes later I decided that, although *Joseph Young* was being tossed around quite violently by the rough seas, she seemed to be handling herself safely, so with foul-weather gear and safety harness still on I crawled under the chart table and fell asleep.

Fifteen days out and I felt completely content, making about 6 knots to a moderate southerly breeze — the first real wind in about four days. Running in to the top of the Azores high-pressure weather system, I had been virtually becalmed for three days—the most frustrating experience imaginable. It was a good thing I was alone and had no witnesses to my outbursts of anger at the lack of progress. The sails flapped from side to side as the boat rolled; one night all sail had to be dropped just so I could get some sleep free of the sound of slatting dacron — a sound guaranteed to drive even the most patient sailor insane. The weather forecasts from the Britain talked of another large high over northern Europe bringing calms and light easterly winds over the approaches to the English Channel for the next several days. I had to psych myself up for a slow finish.

Day 20. *Noon position today puts me north and slightly west of the Scilly Isles. Progress has been painfully slow the last few days with light easterlies as promised by the forecast. I had hoped to make land today, but with the present weather it could be another two days yet. I am somewhat nervous too; closing the coast with this fickle wind and no engine, it would be easy to make a mistake. A good round of stars tonight would go a long way towards reassuring me. With the uncertain currents in this area, having to rely on intermittent fixes from the sun is less than reassuring. Being so low to the water I am acutely aware how close the visible horizon is too. I will be lucky to see land at four miles. Angling down from the north-west, I am hoping for a landfall on Longships Lighthouse.*

14

Day 21. *Altered course to the south shortly after noon to avoid a large tanker steaming north into the Irish Sea. A comforting sight, as noon showed me crossing the northbound traffic lane between Land's End and the Seven Stones. The wind is northerly at Force 3 and am beam-reaching* [sailing with the wind blowing at right angles to the boat's course] *at 6-7 knots. Hope to fetch Longships before sunset. I can barely contain my excitement at the anticipated landfall.*

At 1645 hours, sitting in the cockpit, coffee in hand, a red light winks at me out of the haze on the port bow. Holding myself in check long enough to confirm its characteristic [an identifying sequence of flashes], *I drop quickly below to study the chart. It is in fact Pendeen Light, about five miles north along the coast from Longships. Back on deck I change course to the south, and fifteen minutes later Longships too is visible just off the port bow. Fantastic! If the wind holds I'll be ashore for breakfast.*

Day 22. *Rounding the Lizard last night at 2235 the wind veered to the north-east and increased to Force 6, kicking up an uncomfortable sea. Holding my course I sail on towards the east until 0130 hours. With visibility down to less than two miles in drizzle I want a bit of distance between me and the lee shore on the port side for the last fifteen-mile run up to Falmouth. Rounding on to the starboard tack finally, we're moving along at a good 6 knots. It is 0305 hours before I first see the flash of St. Anthony's Lighthouse, which guards the entrance to Falmouth harbour. By 0400 I am safely in the lee of the bay, slowly dodging back and forth, waiting for daylight before heading into the harbour and up the river to a mooring. Patches of mist slowly running off the land give me cause for real concern and I only hope they burn off with the rising sun. As the sky gradually brightens my grandfather's old house becomes visible up on the overlooking cliffs, and I feel like we're almost home. Time for one last pot of coffee before it's all over.*

Looking back over the last three weeks I don't really want it to end. It's a pity one actually has to arrive to realize the satisfaction of having made the trip. I started out not really knowing what to expect, but aware that if I didn't really enjoy it I would be a coward to not admit it. The truth of the matter is, I loved it! August and Newport can't come too soon.

The experiences, hardships, and mistakes of this first Atlantic crossing and the return voyage to Canada in the spring, with my close friend John Sandford along as crew, were to prove invaluable. Exactly how valuable I was not to find out until faced with real disaster some sixteen months and 17,000 nautical miles later, in the lonely wastes of the southern ocean.

PART ONE

Newport to Cape Town

This, my stomach tells me, is the enemy. In front of me sits a gently steaming plate of eggs, steak, sausages, fries, and tomatoes, complemented by orange juice, coffee, and rolls. A loud ripple of laughter—perhaps a little forced?—echoes around the room. I feel sick.

It is the morning of August 30, 1986. Inside the Goat Island Marina Pub I am sharing a "competitors only" breakfast with twenty-four other men from around the world. The truly international group is comprised of five Frenchmen, nine Americans, two South Africans, a Brazilian, two Australians, a New Zealander, two Finns, a Japanese, an Englishman, and myself, the lone Canadian. It will be almost two months before I again sit down for a meal with another human being. In a scant eight hours all of us around this table will be alone aboard our yachts, racing across the waters of the North Atlantic Ocean. Our common destination will be the port of Cape Town, South Africa, some 7,000 miles to the south-east. This will be the first of four legs in the BOC single-handed around-the-world yacht race. Six of the twenty-five of us here this morning will not make it to the start of the second leg.

I had arrived in Newport, Rhode Island, some three weeks previously, sailing down from Halifax with a crew composed of my brother David and two close friends, Steve Murch and John Sandford. The trip down the coast had provided a good shakedown after a hectic summer spent working round-the-clock to ready the boat for the upcoming voyage. All in all I had been entirely satisfied with the general performance of *Joseph Young*, but the frantic pace of the last two months had taken its toll. Hustling (unsuccessfully) to obtain last-minute sponsorship, putting affairs in order for my long absence, dealing with doubting Thomases, and trying to come to terms with an extended separation from loved ones had left me feeling drained. I needed some time alone with the boat to gather myself for what was yet to come, and I looked forward to the period of relative peace between my arrival and the start of the race.

Two days after arriving in Newport I saw the last of my crew off on a bus to Canada. I was alone. *Joseph Young* was securely berthed at the public wharf alongside *Skoiern IV*, the French yacht to be sailed by Jacques de Roux. Tied up directly in front of us were two other entrants, *Neptune's Express*, skippered by New Zealander Dick McBride, and Jean-Luc Van Den Heede's *Let's Go*, from France. Casting surreptitious glances at the other yachts while I worked on the installation of a spotlight aboard *Joseph Young* I couldn't entirely quell a feeling of envy. They all looked faster and more comfortable than my boat, and were festooned with equipment that I could only dream about. To boot, I saw myself as a rank amateur, rubbing shoulders with sailors whose exploits I admired immensely. I comforted myself with the axiom "simple is safe," thought of the solid way in which *Joseph Young* had behaved during the two Atlantic crossings, and reiterated my commitment to finish what I had started.

Early the following morning I made my way across to Goat Island to meet with members of the Race Committee and arrange for my safety inspection, the last official hurdle before being accepted as a certified competitor. Instant panic! I discovered that the Scrutineering Committee had a long checklist of equipment to be carried by each yacht, copies of which had supposedly been sent to competitors several months in advance. For some reason, my copy had never reached me, and now, reading over the list for the first time, I realized that I was lacking many of the required items. The next two weeks became the mad scramble that I had been hoping to avoid: I trekked around the stores of Newport looking for the equipment needed to satisfy the scrutineers. One item that proved particularily difficult to find was a solar still to convert salt water to fresh. The local surplus store saved the day. For a small price, I purchased there, complete with instructions, an old still (*circa* 1950) once issued to air force pilots flying over the ocean. This unit could produce enough fresh water to substantially delay the agony of death by dehydration, assuming of course that the sea was flat calm and that the sun was beating down mercilessly from a cloudless sky.

Once this last item was safely stowed aboard *Joseph Young* along with the rest of my survival equipment, I welcomed the Scrutineering Committee's inspection and proudly received my competitor's certificate and burgee. I was now officially ready for the start of the race.

The tears run unabated down my face as I watch *Turtles*, the boat carrying my girlfriend, Vicki, my mother, and my close friends turn and scuttle back to the shelter of Newport harbour. The image of that parting will never leave me. It came almost two hours after the starting gun was fired to signal the start of the BOC race, two hours of beating to windward that had left me physically and emotionally exhausted. The large spectator fleet that had massed to watch our departure had overrun the start area, forcing some desperate manoeuvres to avoid collisions and taxing my already strained nerves to breaking point. Now, as I watch *Turtles* fade in the distance I feel very alone.

Joseph Young is close-reaching towards the south-south-east quite comfortably with the windvane steering and except for occasional course alterations to avoid fishing floats I sit motionless in the cockpit, my mind replaying the events of the last ten hours. I can't help but wonder whether I have chosen a wise course for my life to follow for the next ten months, and how all I have left behind will change during my absence. But a mental kick in the behind puts such thoughts aside and I try to concentrate on the job at hand. The proximity of fishing vessels and commercial traffic guarantees a long night ahead, and I decide that a pot of coffee is in order. I clamber down the hatch — jerkily; I haven't yet acquired my sea legs — and brace myself in front of the galley to find the percolator already filled and ready to go. Vicki, aware of my caffeine addiction, has left this as a parting gesture. I feel the tears start up again. While below I take time to plot the most recent fix from the satellite navigator and confirm my progress on the chart. It will be reassuring to have Block Island astern and nothing but open ocean stretching out ahead before sunset. A wealth of "good luck" cards from friends covers the navigation area, and as I'm searching for a plastic bag to keep them in, I hear the unmistakable "whup-whup-whup" of an approaching helicopter. Scrambling up on deck to see what the excitement is about, I spot *Credit Agricole*, a French yacht, about half a mile to the west of me, apparently heading back towards Newport. Philippe Jeantot (who won the last BOC race in 1982) is visible on the bow, wrestling with a partially hoisted headsail. There is obviously a problem of some sort, but my attention quickly transfers to the chopper (one of several press helicopters that had been buzzing around at the start), which begins to circle around *Joseph Young* just a bit too close for comfort. I don't like these noisy intruders spying on me, they don't even decrease my loneliness, and I am glad when it finally turns and races back to the action at *Credit Agricole*. As I watch, the sixty-footer turns and resumes a course parallel to mine, heading back southwards towards Cape Town. Philippe has evidently decided to carry on. I'm glad, but the speed with which his boat overhauls me does nothing for my lagging spirits.

My basic plan for the first leg is to clear the Gulf Stream, pass Bermuda just to the west, and then reach across the north-east trade winds to cross the doldrums, the area near the equator known for its calms or light winds, close to its western limits. *Joseph Young* loves to broad reach, and I am hoping that by not heading too much towards the east until we're farther south in the trades, I can help her show the speed I know she is capable of. Not knowing what strategy the other Class-Two competitors have decided upon makes me somewhat anxious; in a lot of ways it would be "safer" to try and stay with the fleet and thus share the same sailing conditions, but I need a lucky long shot to make up for my lack of size; being one of the three smallest boats in the race (and the smallest to actually finish) means in theory that we should also be the slowest.

By seven o'clock this first evening the once brisk southerly wind has eased slightly and the single reef I have been carrying in the main needs to be shaken out. I welcome the brief flurry of activity. I am enjoying the feeling of finally being on my way. *Joseph Young* continues to move well, and unless the wind drops further, it won't be necessary to change the #3 jib for a larger headsail. Around the rapidly darkening horizon the lights of numerous fishing boats are easily seen. I wonder where the rest of the competitors are.

The wind does continue to drop, and by eleven o'clock it is obvious that the small #3 jib must be replaced by the larger #2. Changing headsails alone, even under the best of conditions, involves thirty minutes of hard labour. It is always easy to procrastinate, but I goad myself with thoughts of the other boats charging ahead of me and clip my safety harness on to the jack-stay, after making sure a pair of pliers are tucked in the pocket of my foul-weather gear. The halyard, the line that raises and lowers the sail, is prepared for quick release. The procedure is to let the halyard go, and then scramble up to the bow before the entire sail slides down the forestay and is washed overboard. If you don't get to the bow in time, you face the hernia-inducing prospect of hauling the whole sodden mess back on deck. All goes smoothly this time, however, and within half an hour the #2 is up and properly trimmed. Back in the cockpit, I notice that the lights of the fishing vessels have slipped over the horizon and I have the whole wide expanse of ocean and sky to myself. My first night at sea is an absolutely beautiful one; the sky is clear and spangled with thousands of stars. Huddled on deck, I drift in and out of sleep, waking to check for other ships, seeing none, and rocking back into my dreams.

My fitful rest ends at five in the morning with the noise of the mainsail flogging. The wind has all but died, and the wind-vane self-steering has given up, allowing the boat to come into the wind. The sun has not yet fully risen and in the half-light of dawn the I stow away the #2, which I have replaced with the drifter, a very large, light headsail ideal for such conditions. When things on deck are once again shipshape, my thoughts turn to breakfast.

I had kept the cooking arrangements aboard *Joseph Young* simple for reasons of both safety and reliability; all my meals were to be prepared on a two-burner alcohol stove. Firmly wedged between the galley sink and the companionway ladder, with my feet braced against the boat's motion, it is possible to reach almost anything in the galley without having to take a step. One advantage to a small boat! Within ten minutes my first culinary masterpiece of the race is ready for the eating: bacon, eggs, toast, and, of course, coffee—a fine start to my first full day at sea.

With the drifter exchanged for the spinnaker we make about 4 knots on a south-easterly heading. The wind shifts around at seven-thirty to blow light but steady from the north, making it necessary to gybe onto the port tack and steer a little more towards the east. The weather is absolutely perfect, an almost flat sea disturbed only by a low easy swell, and not a trace of cloud to break the sun's warmth. The barometer has been edging its way down since early yesterday evening, an encouraging sign that the wind will not quit entirely. Moving around the deck, trimming sails and occasionally taking a spell at the tiller, I am more than content. The peace and tranquillity of the sea's mood is a welcome tonic after the frenzy of Newport. I am where I want to be.

At noon I take our position and find that we have covered 139 miles since crossing the starting line. I feel optimistic that the gentle breeze is helping *Joseph Young* make some distance over the larger, heavier boats in Class Two. Munching on a lunch of cheese and crackers I read over the Race Instructions for the first leg and make note of the radio frequencies for the afternoon "chat hour." Reprogramming the sideband radio for the correct channels will be first on the agenda for this afternoon, a job that I simply did not have time for in port. The chat hour is a time when all participants can discuss problems, exchange weather information, and offer each other encouragement. I am eagerly looking forward to this first contact with the other boats at sea, anxious to hear how they are faring in the present weather conditions.

By four in the afternoon I am in front of the radio, coffee in hand, ready for news of the others. The afternoon has passed quickly, the calm seas affording a great opportunity to clean the boat and restow tools, clothing, and other items more securely for the rougher weather that surely lies ahead. Some of the least-used sails I transferred from the forepeak to the aft lockers to make sail-handling a little easier and to improve the trim of the boat. All in all, a very satisfactory few hours. Suddenly the radio comes to life: *Lone Star* (Mark Schrader) is calling *American Flag* (Hal Roth). I listen in to their short conversation and find that they seem to have much the same wind conditions as I do. I can't help feeling a little relieved. After Mark and Hal sign off, New Zealander Dick McBride calls me, and I am able to pass some frequencies to him for the weather facsimile stations that cover this area. Dick's position puts him about thirty-five miles to the east of me, so I am not doing too badly.

Radio contact with the other competitors leaves me in a good mood, dispelling somewhat my feeling of being all alone out here. I set to making supper with renewed enthusiasm. Following the meal, the day's dishes are tossed into a bucket and I clamber topside for the odious chore of dishwashing. Lacking a salt-water pump to the galley sink, and being a little concerned about the fresh-water supply on this first leg, I will do all the washing up on deck. The luxury liner *Queen Elizabeth II*, this is not!

As the sun nears the western horizon a few dolphins appear, perhaps attracted by the sound of our progress through the low swell. Down below, the whistles and squeaks of these most beautiful of sea creatures are clearly audible through the hull. I wonder if their conversation centres on *Joseph Young*, questioning her presence here in their territory.

Before dark, I decide to take down the spinnaker and replace it with the drifter. This will cut our speed a little, but I am not yet comfortable with the idea of carrying a 'chute at night, and I need to get some rest. Once all is sorted out on deck, I slip below to stretch out gratefully on the settee berth. The alarm is set to wake me in two hours' time. Sleep comes easily. My first day alone on the open sea has passed.

September 7, 1986
22 37N 62 00W

One week at sea yesterday. Everything is going well despite a few initial setbacks. A few nights ago five to six feet of stitching on the mainsail let go during a sudden squall. Took several days to repair due to inclement weather and probably cost me a good hundred miles. Also broke one of two light air blades for the windvane self-steering during the same squall.

Not a bad day today though — southerly winds and making about eight knots under singled reefed mainsail and #3 jib. A bit worried by the weather — an earlier facsimile picture showed a real bulge in the isobars to the south-east. Has signs of developing into a tropical storm. (The weather facsimile recorder was lent to me for the race. It consists of a radio receiver connected to a printer, which, when tuned in to designated radio stations, will print out weather maps for most ocean areas.)

After seven days at sea I am 1,175 miles from Newport and very far from being bored. Problems started to develop for me four days ago, only three days after my departure from Newport. (I hope this doesn't indicate the shape of things to come!) In the late hours of the morning I noticed a short tear along one of the seams in the mainsail. The weather was moderate and, lowering the mainsail onto the deck, I was able to replace the six inches of stitching that had let go. A similar problem had occurred on the trip down from Halifax to Newport, and although even then I feared that the sail was near the end of its better days, financial constraints had prevented me from replacing it before I set off. I just hoped that it would last for the duration of the leg.

About an hour after I got the sail back up and drawing, I was scanning the horizon when my shocked eyes sighted a sail off to the north-north-west. Hardly able to contain my excitement, I dove below for the binoculars. Although I could not be positive, the boat looked like Mark Schrader's *Lone Star*. Infected with race fever, I spent the next eleven hours coaxing *Joseph Young* to her maximum speed, determined not to let Mark slip by me during the night. But, by two in the morning the call of the pillow was too strong to ignore, and I crawled into my sleeping bag, first tucking a single reef in the mainsail due to the frequent squalls passing through the area. Three short hours later I was rudely awakened by the sound of flogging dacron, and was sickened to discover another, this time more serious, tear in the mainsail.

With the sail down on the deck again, I faced double stitching about five feet of heavy dacron. This would take considerable time. Although the damage was obviously repairable, I couldn't help feeling depressed. Sitting on the cabin top, surrounded by yards of sailcloth, cursing as I continually jabbed the needle into my still soft fingertips, I thought of the ground I must be losing to the other boats. Good fortune, I felt, was surely not on my side.

It took me three days to complete repairs on the mainsail, but on the afternoon of the second day, September 4, I was given good reason to stop feeling sorry for myself.

Tuning in to the chat hour that day I was shocked to hear that *Airforce*, another Class-Two entrant, had sunk that morning. She had collided with a waterlogged shipping container during the early hours of the morning, forcing her skipper, Dick Cross, to abandon her and take to the liferaft. Fortunately, a helicopter flying out of Bermuda had responded to his call, and Dick was safely ashore within a matter of hours.

Sitting below with a mug of cocoa later that night, I was unable to shake a creeping fear brought on by that afternoon's news. Despite the best of planning, the most meticulous of preparations, luck, I realized, had each one of us within her grasp. I tried to imagine how Dick had felt, how I would feel, watching a dream being torn away. It would be, I decided, unbearable.

By midnight that night, cocooned in my sleeping bag, I was cheered by the knowledge that Bermuda, the last solid obstacle between *Joseph Young* and the equator, was safely behind me. The wind had increased to gale force shortly after dark, and the motion became violent as we drove to windward under shortened sail. Foolishly, considering the fact that I carried no detailed charts of the area, I had passed very close to the island at ten o'clock. Loath to tack to the south-west and risk giving up more ground to the other boats, I had actually sighted the loom of the lighthouse off to the east. With lightning intermittently ripping across the sky, it had been eerie to see the weak man-made beam sweeping the low cloud far on the horizon with such regularity. If a choice was being offered, mine had been made. My destination lay far to the south.

During the next four days I felt a subtle but distinct change in my feelings about my solitary position out here. Gone are the mental pressures brought about by the frantic start and the navigational headaches of clearing Bermuda and picking a fair course to the equator. All around me lies nothing but thousands of square miles of uninterrupted ocean. I accept that I exist in the physical world as no more than a minuscule insignificant dot. It brings me a feeling of contentment I have never found in any other way.

September 11, 1986
22 18N 55 15W
Last night was awful.

Managed two one-hour-long sleeps in between trying to keep the boat moving. The wind was all over the place and often light, and with the swell that was running the sails were unable to hold the wind, slapping loudly to and fro as we rolled. Squalls and lightning came and went just to keep it interesting. I was really in need of sleep too — my temper flared at the slightest little things, and I'm glad there were no witnesses to my violent outbursts of colourful language.

Wind filled in from the south-south-west this morning at about 0730 and I changed to the #2 jib. About ninety minutes later the wind picked up rapidly and in quick succession I was forced to tuck in three reefs and change down to the #4 jib. Been making over 8 knots to weather all day and feeling quite smug! Suspected a tropical disturbance to the east and was going south to get around on the navigable side. After talking with Mark on Lone Star *I feel lucky.*

Mark is running to the north-east under bare poles in 50 knots of wind, gusting 60, so I'm making good time on him. Cruel of me, but I'm hoping the boys farther east are in the light winds showing on the weather facsimile picture.

Cooked a big cheese and onion omelette with fresh tomatoes for "brunch." All out of bread now so will have to get up the enthusiasm to cook bannock.

Weather on deck is still bad — water going everywhere and motion fairly uncomfortable. Have had a splitting headache all day despite taking several pain-killers.

Must lie down for an hour as I fully expect the wind to drop off tonight and more sail will be needed. Takes a real mental kick to keep in the racing mood. I find the Argos satellite-tracking beacon [which the Race Committee had installed on each yacht in the race] *to be a real incentive for me to try and to keep the boat moving. When I think of John Sandford plotting the Argos positions on the wall chart at the Dartmouth Yacht Club, I realize that everybody will know if I'm being lazy.*

Some sparrow-like bird landed on deck this afternoon. Poor thing looks absolutely beat, and will probably be dead by morning, despite my attempts to feed him water and crackers.

Normally I dislike birds, but this incident with the sparrow moved me tremendously. Perhaps it was the fact of physical contact with another living creature after having spent so many days alone; perhaps it was sympathy for the creature's plight. Blown out to sea by an offshore wind and aware that landing on the sea meant death, the poor bird must have seen *Joseph Young*, solid, dry, and signalling the end of an exhausting struggle to stay aloft, as heaven-sent. It made no attempt to circle, but came straight in for a belly-landing on the starboard side of the coachroof. There it lay, its whole body pumping in time with its heart, and we stared unblinkingly at one another. Moving slowly I slipped below to fetch an offering of fresh water and crumbled crackers, but the bird seemed totally uninterested. By nightfall its beak was down, resting on the deck to support its head. I did not hold out much hope for its survival.

In the morning I quietly dropped the stiffened, cold little body overboard, saddened that the lonely struggle had ended in an environment so foreign.

I would find out some weeks later, after managing to place a radio-telephone call through to Vicki, that the strong breeze that had helped me log my first 200-mile day of the trip was generated by Hurricane Earl. Fortunately I had been able to get to the south of the hurricane's eye before it passed to the northeast of me. Mark Schrader, as I noted in my journal, had been closer to the storm's centre, and had been forced to run off before the wind with all sail dropped. I was also disturbed to learn that official race reports (received by Vicki, my family, and friends at home) had placed me in "the most dangerous quadrant" of the hurricane. It bothered me that anxiety at home was being heightened by such misinformation. Of course, I had known before I left that the race would be harder, mentally, for those left behind. The uncertainty of not knowing exactly what was happening from day to day would leave their imaginations free to conjure up all sorts of horror stories. With radio-telephone links being both expensive and sporadic, there was little I could do to lay those sorts of fears to rest.

Following this brush with Hurricane Earl, three days of fair sailing ensued, with respectable daily runs keeping me in good spirits. The hoped-for north-east trade winds still hadn't materialized, and with the breeze from the east my only concern was that I was forced to stay on this too southerly course. *Joseph Young* did not mind though, and forged resolutely onward, throwing cascades of spray back over the weather rail as she knifed through waves, always nipping at the magic two-hundred-mile day.

My physical suffering during these days was limited to a blistering sunburn on both cheeks. I had decided one fateful afternoon that a little nude sunbathing wouldn't be out of order so, after a quick check of the horizon, I doffed my shorts and settled down on deck. When I awoke an hour or so later it was already too late. For the next few days, sitting down was an exercise in pure masochism.

31

The heat was made bearable only by the constant breeze, and I took to making tea in my largest saucepan in an attempt to slake my constant thirst. The technique was simple; boil water in saucepan, add two teabags, stir in one cup of milk (made from powder), remove teabags, transfer entire contents of saucepan to stomach via throat. With practice, the entire operation could be completed in less than half an hour.

For September 16, my log showed a noon-to-noon run of 193 miles, with 914 miles to go before I crossed the equator and headed into the Southern Hemisphere. I didn't know it at the time, but it was the end of a rather pleasant two weeks and the beginning of ten days of absolute frustration, mental anguish, and exhaustion.

Lying just to the north of the equator, spanning some four hundred miles in a north/south direction, lies an area of the Atlantic that has been the bane of sailors' lives for centuries. Lying between the trade winds of the North and South Atlantic this zone of low pressure is characterized by its long, hot, windless days, broken only by frequent and violent thunderstorms of short duration. To pass through this meteorological divide while relying only on the power of the wind to propel one's vessel is to enter into a game of chance with Mother Nature herself. This area is known simply as the doldrums.

At two o'clock on the afternoon of September 16 I was on deck, hand-steering in an easterly wind of Force 6, *Joseph Young* clipping along at about 8 knots. For the last hour I had been apprehensively eyeing a long line of very black cloud to the south of me. Lightning was clearly visible within the clouds, turning the black to a dark grey as it rippled from cloud to cloud. Closer now, a curtain of rain was drawn between the clouds and the sea. With no way around, I waited for the squall line to hit, shivers of trepidation running up and down my spine.

I sailed into the darkness, gripping the tiller with whitened knuckles, and the rain struck with unbelievable ferocity. It came down in absolute torrents, reducing visibility to a scant hundred feet, but mercifully dropping the temperature and giving me a thorough fresh-water bath! Incredibly and suddenly, the wind dropped to nothing. I was totally becalmed. *Joseph Young* rolled helplessly, the sails slapping, as I glanced nervously around waiting for a sudden wind shift and damaging squalls. Nothing. After ten minutes, the rain stopped just as suddenly as it had begun, and a light southerly breeze filled in under an overcast sky. Moving again, albeit slowly, we crept off to the east for the next few hours. After we had covered six or eight miles, the wind backed quickly to the east, resumed blowing at a steady Force 5, and after a somewhat sloppy tack, we were once again heading in the right direction at speed.

Things seemed to be fine again. I opened the last can of chicken for supper and enjoyed a fine feed of curry and rice. Over a pot of tea I wrote another page of a long letter home and brought the log-book up to date. Before turning in I crawled back up on deck and shook out a reef in the mainsail, the wind having dropped a notch since nightfall. But things were not fine.

September 19, 1986
09 56N 43 15W

The last forty-eight hours have been hellish. Am feeling fairly depressed tonight — if it wasn't for an encouraging chat with Bertie Reed aboard Stabilo Boss *and the fact that I managed to sneak by Mac Smith on* Quailo *last night, things would really be bad. The wind has been all over the place and always very light. Had about four hours' sleep last night and was hand-steering the boat for the reminder of the day. Occasional heavy rain showers with violent squalls and rapid wind shifts. Only covered ninety-five miles noon-to-noon, while the boys off to the east are romping along.*

All the eggs I tried for breakfast this morning were rotten, so I threw out the last half dozen and had corned beef hash, home fries, and baked beans. Drank about a gallon of tea today — hope the water supply lasts.

After writing these few lines, I fell asleep at the chart table, exhausted by the heat, angered and frustrated by the fickle wind, tired of having my adrenalin pumped up by violent squalls only to be left windless a few minutes later.

I awoke with a start at midnight as *Joseph Young* was slammed unmercifully by yet another squall, thrown almost on her beam ends as the sails were taken aback. Silly with sleep, I dragged myself up through the hatch and back into the fray, instantly soaked by the pelting rain. Shouting loudly over the noise of the wind and the sails, cursing generations of boat-builders, race organizers, wind gods, and oceans, I ordered myself through the performance of making the situation safe. Free the jib sheets, disconnect the self-steering, grind on the windward runner, let go the leeward runner, ease the traveller, reset the steering, crawl forward and drop the jib, trim the main, tidy the jib sheets. With everything once again secure, fully awake, it's back down below to dry off and make some coffee, sit out the squall, and wait for the opportunity to hoist more sail. These conditions would plague me for the next five days, often limiting sleep to several short naps during the cooler nights.

September 24, 1986
05 07N 36 38W

I'm keeping my fingers firmly crossed but it would seem that I finally escaped the clutches of the doldrums this morning at about 0300. Yesterday just about did me in mentally; after seven days of rolling around with rarely enough breeze to stop the sails slatting I became finally and absolutely becalmed. To add to the enjoyment, Joseph Young *had come to rest sitting in a slick of diesel oil.*

Was down below yesterday afternoon having a coffee, out of the sun's glare, when I heard a muted rumbling through the boat's hull. Looking out of the porthole, I saw a large Brazilian trawler coming to a crash stop about four hundred feet off my starboard side! Frightened, I quickly turned on the VHF *radio and heard him calling me. It took some time for me to convince him all was okay on board. He had sighted* Joseph Young *from a distance and, seeing the headsail down on deck and nobody in sight, he was preparing to lower a boat and send away a boarding party when I finally responded. After thanking him for his concern and diligence, we wished each other a fair voyage and he drew away, disappearing rapidly over the horizon. I must confess that when I first saw the other vessel almost alongside, piracy was the thought uppermost in my mind.*

Calm continued throughout more torrential rain last night and I dropped all sail and went to sleep in disgust, setting the alarm to wake me every two hours.

Since sunrise I've had light east-south-east wind. The

improvement in my temper is remarkable. Once again, the radio chats with Mark Schrader, Mac Smith, and Bertie Reed have kept us all sane: misery loves company!

September 26, 1986
04 47N 35 08W
Lowered sail at 0200 this morning, after being becalmed all day, in an attempt to get some peace, free of the sound of slatting sails. Up again at 0630 and still no wind. Had a simple breakfast of cold cereal and coffee, and finally at 0745 light easterly zephyrs started appearing. Hoisted full sail and took my place at the tiller, managing a scant 1.5 knots through the water. With the current setting us to the north-east I'm not exactly optimistic about our progress.

Wind shifted to the east-south-east and picked up slightly at 1000 hours. Thankfully just enough speed now for the windvane self-steering to control the boat, freeing me from the tedious job at the helm. Just before the wind arrived I experienced a short, sharp swell from the west, with the crests breaking into the breeze. Very strange. Accompanied for almost half an hour by several dolphins and some birds. Hope this was my welcoming committee to the south-east trade winds.

September 27, 1986
02 40N 35 07W
Finally got good steady south-east trades last night. Hard to believe, but Mac on Quailo, *lying 60 miles to the west of me, and Mark on* Lone Star, *40 miles to the east of me, both came into the same wind twenty-two to thirty-six hours before I did! That puts me approximately 60 miles behind Mark, and an incredible 150 miles behind Mac. It will be very difficult to make up that kind of ground in the twenty-five days or so remaining before we arrive in Cape Town. The boats out to the east are all moving along nicely too. My only real hope for a good placing on this first leg now is for the South Atlantic high-pressure weather system to fill in to the east, as the bulk of the Class-Two fleet are nearly four days closer to port than I am.*

A busy day aboard Joseph Young. *Opening the port cockpit locker to get fuel for the stove I discovered it was full to the brim with water. Quickly tasted it—very brackish but definitely not sea water, thank goodness; probably a result of all the heavy rain over the last week. After pumping the locker dry, I cut and glued on a new rubber gasket. Unfortunately the spare engine filters stored in that locker are now all ruined.*

Also found fresh water leaking from under the starboard settee. It stopped after a few minutes, so whether it is coming from the fresh-water tank or is merely accumulated condensation is difficult to determine.

I am slightly worried by the drinking-water situation. Am consuming vast quantities of tea in this hot weather and hope the eighty-gallon supply lasts me until Cape Town. I must try and collect rain water whenever the opportunity presents itself.

The log has also started giving rather erratic readings. Removed and examined the connections behind the switchboard but found no obvious faults. Without accurate instruments, it is hard to get the most out of the boat.

Being out of the doldrums and into the trade winds was a drastic change, mentally and physically. Gone was the maddening heat and fickle weather, but after a week it seemed that even the trades were part of some grand scheme to wear me down. Day after day, mile after mile, we ground away on the port tack, *Joseph Young* heeled well over to starboard, bumping, pounding, and slamming as she shouldered aside the endless train of oncoming waves. A continuous light spray soon coated the entire boat and contents with a fine layer of salt; every cloth, towel, and bunk cushion felt gritty and damp to the touch. My hair developed the texture of fine steel wool, and attempts to brush the salt from around my eyes invariably led to a bout of tears and frantic blinking in an effort to stop the stinging.

The expression "rubbing salt in the wound" never seemed more appropriate. After escaping the clutches of the North Atlantic, I could not help feeling that my dues had been paid, and I had looked forward longingly to a landfall in South Africa. However, after crossing the equator on September 28 I was only a scant 175 miles beyond the halfway point. I could look forward to a second nearly full month at sea. The first leg was by no means over.

I rose early on the morning of October 6, prepared to enjoy perhaps the finest day's sailing I would experience during my transit of the South Atlantic. My spirits were buoyed by the previous evening's radio-telephone call to Vicki to a degree that is difficult to imagine. These too-infrequent contacts with home were occasions to be anticipated, savoured, and recalled over and over again. They reminded me that although I was alone in my immediate physical world, my mental and emotional world was very full.

On deck, the weather was perfect. The wind had eased and backed slightly, making for a more comfortable ride, and the sun was shining from an almost cloudless sky. However, as I looked aloft, part of a daily routine of checking the rig and sails, I realized that my perfect day was not off to the best of starts. The port checkstay had parted during the night, and half of it now lay trailing over the stern of the boat, while the other half was still attached to the mast. Although not absolutely essential for supporting the mast, the checkstay was needed to keep the rig in racing trim. I pulled the broken length of wire from the water and sat back for a minute. As I contemplated the situation, I realized that the next step, quite obviously, would be to climb the mast and retrieve the fitting and short length of wire now swinging around some twenty-five feet above my head. Although I seriously doubted my chances of making a suitable repair, I was concerned about the possibility of the jagged strands of wire tearing the mainsail.

After making sure that I had the necessary tools for the job securely attached to my belt, I cautiously shinnied up the port side of the mast until I could swing my legs over the lower spreaders. Sitting there for a moment to catch my breath I was pleasantly surprised at how easy it had been. None the less, the motion of the boat was magnified by height, and I couldn't quite dispel the picture of myself being pitched cleanly through the air to watch *Joseph Young* sail alone into the distance before I consigned myself to my watery grave. I found that if I stood on the spreader, I could just reach the checkstay fitting. With one hand wielding the screwdriver and one hand holding on to the mast, I was thankful when the retaining plate finally came free, allowing me to remove the broken end. Descending to the deck to examine the fitting, I felt more than a little satisfied, almost smug, with my high-wire prowess. It was fairly evident that the failure had been caused by the wire kinking where it attached to the mast fitting, and I resolved to change all similar fittings in Cape Town to guard against any further problems.

Having skipped breakfast, I decided to tackle a curry for lunch; corned beef and chopped onion on rice. The result bore an uncanny resemblance to a bowl of rather poor-quality dog food, but mast-climbing is hungry work; I wolfed it down. The day before I had made my first batch of pan bread or bannock, and had eaten the whole lot before it had a chance to cool down. Spread thickly with margarine and honey it was like manna from heaven. The pleasures in my life have become very simple.

That evening I sat at the small desk in the cabin enjoying a mug of cocoa and writing a letter to Vicki. The early hours of darkness became my favourite time during these weeks of steady sailing. Above, an almost unbroken canopy of stars follows closely upon the setting of the sun, and the temperature drops enough to make it comfortable down below. Lit by a single reading lamp, the cabin becomes a cosy oasis in the vast emptiness of the ocean. Thoughts come easily to paper.

I had been struck in recent days by the nature of the conversations passing back and forth on the chat hour. We had left Newport almost six weeks ago, a group of strangers, seen by many, I am sure, as hard-bitten sailors with a questionable grip on sanity and a penchant for being alone. But now, time on the airwaves is taken up with the exchange of recipes for eking out dwindling supplies of food and making our monotonous meals more palatable. We share schemes for wrangling airfares from prospective sponsors to fly wives and sweethearts to the upcoming stopover. Encouragement is offered to those feeling down and bonds form among us as we undergo our common self-imposed ordeal.

Sometime that night, during the hours of darkness, I passed to the westward of Islas de Trinidade, the last close piece of land before I reach the continent of Africa. Only three weeks to port. Come on *Joseph Young*!

October 8, 1986
23 05S 26 46W
A long night last night with light winds from midnight on. Too little boat speed for the windvane self-steering to be reliable (it seems that this wind-driven device needs enough wind to keep the boat moving at least 4 knots before it can steer a proper course), requiring a hand on the tiller to keep on course. Managed two hours' sleep, sitting fully dressed on the quarterberth, during a brief period of steady breeze.

Had an experience last night that will stay with me forever. I was sitting on deck with the inevitable mug of cocoa at 0230, having just hoisted the drifter in place of the #1. The moon was reflected on an almost calm sea, the sky only partly cloudy. Suddenly, off to the north-east the darkness was broken by a bright flame. Looking quickly over my shoulder to port made my scalp tingle. A meteorite was falling rapidly and silently through the night sky. For a crazy instant I actually thought it might hit me, it seemed so close! Mesmerized, I watched, and the image of its passing — streaming a long tail of flame, shedding glowing lumps of debris as it fell — was seared on my memory. I actually winced as it met the horizon, anticipating an explosion to mark the end of its short life. There was only silence.

Though I'm not one to believe in signs, the meteor's fall was so awe-inspiring that my thoughts turned to my brother Tom, three years younger than me, who was at this moment training on jets with the Canadian Air Force. It took great willpower to stop myself from dashing to the radio and trying to call home.

The wind has remained light to moderate today. Saw my first shark this afternoon, about fifteen feet long. It made a lazy circle of

40

the boat before disappearing. Exercised a little extra caution while rinsing the coffee pot over the side.

Scissored and shaved off the scruffy beginnings of a beard today and had a salt-water shower on deck. Feel like a new man.

With the passing of October's first week I said good-bye to the relatively pleasant weather of the lower latitudes. From here to Cape Town we would be sailing under the influence of the frontal systems passing eastward across the reaches of the southern oceans. As we were to discover, the first leg was far from over.

Inwardly cursing I fought to gain control over yards of wet, flapping sailcloth. I gasped as another wave broke over the bow, burying me up to the waist and sending a heavy shower of cold water over my head and shoulders. Ten minutes ago I had been sleeping soundly in the quarterberth, cocooned in the warmth of an almost-dry sleeping bag. Predictably, the weather had decided to change shortly after I had turned in, the wind rising rapidly from a light breeze to near gale force.

It was a forty-minute struggle before the drifter was down, the #3 jib up and drawing, and two reefs tucked in the main, but by 0200, *Joseph Young* was properly trimmed once again and moving well. I wasn't surprised to note that the wind was from the south-east, the very direction in which I wanted to go. Faced with the choice of steering either south or east, I opted to tack and go east, at least for the time being. That accomplished, it was back down below to towel off and dress warmly for what promised to be another long night.

An hour and a half later I was once again up on the foredeck changing headsails. The wind and sea had continued to build, and a further reduction in the amount of sail I could safely carry was called for. I was now down to the small #4 jib and a fully reefed main, and hoping against all odds that the wind would moderate or at least change direction. It was simply maddening to be sailing swiftly (and with some discomfort) to windward, knowing all the time that I was not even making miles in the right direction.

By early afternoon the headsail had to be taken down altogether to reduce speed. *Joseph Young* was taking an awful beating, launching herself off the oncoming waves to drop heavily down into the trough with an almighty splash. Life on board had plummeted to a new low. The bouncing was physically exhausting; even the simplest of jobs became a major chore. My hips, elbows, and knees were bruised from trying to brace myself while freeing my hands to work the boat. Even my supper that evening was less than appetizing. I had brought along a supply of boil-in-the-bag meals, pre-cooked foods in foil pouches that required only a few minutes in boiling water to render them edible. At times like this, when the roller-coaster ride made preparing a normal meal almost impossible, they were a godsend. Boiled in fresh water into which a couple of tea bags were thrown, they made possible a hot meal and a mug-up within fifteen minutes, an essential pick-me-up when the going was tough.

After supper came the radio chat hour. I contacted Mark Schrader on *Lone Star*, hoping that sharing our discomfort would help me feel a little less sorry for myself. Mark casually mentioned that he had just emerged from a hot shower only to find that his snifter of brandy was slightly over-warmed. My eyes glazed over. Perhaps, I suggested coolly, a serving hatch installed between the shower and the galley (obviously an oversight on the part of the builder) would help prevent further such uncivilized occurrences. Both Mark and I were a little surprised that Mac Smith on *Quailo* did not come up on the air, but put it down to the weather. Mac was a few hundred miles to the south-south-west of us, and was likely experiencing the same conditions as we were, if not slightly worse.

The gale continued unabated the following day, and I was disappointed to realize that the other boats were pulling away from me. I had worked very hard since emerging from the clutches of the doldrums to close the gap with some of the other Class-Two boats, but the present weather was simply not in my favour. Pondering the overall situation, I saw that my outlook on the race had to change. This I expressed in a letter written to Vicki later that night.

Things here are okay, albeit progress is painfully slow. The last forty-eight hours have changed my mental attitude quite a bit, at least as far as this first leg is concerned. Have a full gale of wind from the south-east (exactly the direction I want to go!) and can't press the boat too hard. Am making about five and a half knots, and even then

*it's rough. I had managed to close to within thirty-five miles of Mark
but with his heavier boat he can take a bit more punishment without
real danger. So — he has left me standing. I guess all along I thought
that if I worked really hard I could manage to keep up with some of
the larger boats, but such is not the case — at least not on this leg.
After being depressed about this for a while and feeling somewhat
defeatist about the whole thing, I actually felt in a good mood today.
As I've told everybody, and must now accept myself, my real goal is
to finish the race safe and sound and to get back to you. If that means
giving up a week or two along the way, that's going to have to be okay.*

On the morning of October 12, I woke early, sensing a change
in the weather. Pulling on damp oilskins, I ventured on deck.
Sure enough, the wind had shifted to the east and moderated
slightly. Grinning contentedly at the improvement, I hoisted the
#4 jib, and tacked, able now to steer a course very close to what
I needed. By seven o'clock everything was shipshape and I went
below for a hot breakfast of baked beans and fried potatoes,
followed by the morning radio schedule. Switching on, I heard
two of the other competitors discussing the sailing conditions a
little farther to the east. Suddenly their conversation was interrupted by the international code for an urgency message, "Pan
Pan, Pan Pan, Pan Pan, the yacht *Quailo* calling any BOC boat.
The yacht *Quailo* calling any BOC boat. Do you read? Over." I
was stunned. Mac was in trouble.

During my career in the Merchant Navy, I had been involved
in distress situations; I had seen people injured, I had seen death
at sea. On each occasion I had tried hard to be professional, to
remain slightly detached while performing a job. This was different. Mac was a friend; he was part of the team. My heart went
out to him.

Responding to his call, I acknowledged the fact that I was
receiving his signal, and asked Mac to transmit his position
before saying anything further. This done, he continued,
describing his present predicament and the events that had
befallen him during the last twenty-four hours.

The gale that *Joseph Young* had struggled through during the last two days had caught *Quailo* with even greater ferocity. Mac described sixty-foot seas and storm-force winds, which had eventually forced him to run off downwind. Trouble with his windvane self-steering had forced him to hand steer for long periods and exhaustion had set in. The need for sleep had become paramount, and, securing the helm, Mac lashed himself in the bunk for a much-needed rest. While he slept, *Quailo* had fallen victim to one of the massive seas boiling up astern. Mac awoke as his boat was hurled right over, rolling through 360 degrees. A few short hours later another wave knocked the yacht down on her side.

Mac, thank goodness, had not been injured and although he sounded badly shaken by the experience, he had a very difficult situation under control. *Quailo* had not fared quite so well. Her mast had been badly bent as some of the rigging was carried away, the self-steering was gone, and, perhaps worst of all, Mac's container of survival gear had broken loose and been swept overboard. Down below, Mac described a scene of absolute chaos, with equipment and floorboards torn loose, and water everywhere. He was also concerned that his Argos beacon had accidentally been activated in the emergency mode and was anxious to inform Race Headquarters that he did not require assistance.

Mark too was talking to Mac and he offered to make any phone calls to shore that might be required. As Mac asked Mark to call his wife and reassure her, his voice broke completely. Listening, I had to fight back tears. Mark and I were able to offer little except words of encouragement, but we agreed to keep a radio watch for as long as Mac felt in need of the contact.

Mac subsequently made a seamanlike passage to Rio de Janeiro, where he reluctantly withdrew from the race. We greatly missed him in Cape Town.

The next thousand miles passed with mostly rough weather, but at least progress was good. Day by day it became harder, mentally, to stay on top. I knew that each day more of the larger boats were arriving in port, and consequently the size of the fleet at sea was rapidly diminishing. Thinking of my fellow competitors stepping ashore to the luxuries of warm, dry beds and good fresh food only increased my impatience to join them. To add to my frustration, radio conditions had repeatedly foiled my attempts to phone Vicki, depriving me of the single most important comfort I had left. As well, an ear infection that had been bothering me for the last few weeks had worsened, making me virtually deaf on one side. The sighting of my first albatross, that graceful wanderer of the sea, would, I hoped, bring the luck that tradition dictated. I felt it was long overdue.

On October 17, I was romping along with a gale-force wind just off the stern. The weather was a little unsettled as a front approached from the west, and frequent squalls with heavy rain kept me on deck trimming sails as the self-steering aimed us towards Cape Town. Surfing down the face of the waves at speed was exciting. I willed away the miles. Cresting the umpteenth wave of the morning I cranked in the sheets as *Joseph Young* picked up her heels and accelerated quickly onto a plane. Looking forward at the jib to check the trim, my eyes were drawn down to the trough of the swell. Transfixed, I gazed in horror, knowing that it was already too late. I could never reach the tiller in time. Directly ahead, its barnacle-encrusted back barely breaking the surface, lay a whale at least as big as my boat. I braced myself for impact, wondering how this leviathan would react to being slammed by 12,000 pounds of lead and plastic travelling at 15 knots. I hoped his temper was less easily aroused than my own.

As the distance between us closed rapidly, the water ahead began to boil. Seconds later, *Joseph Young* careened through this mini-whirlpool with her skipper clinging to the deck. Nothing. In disbelief I peered astern, expecting to see an enraged whale in hot pursuit. Still nothing. Shaking, I let the air out of my lungs, hardly believing my narrow escape. Had he heard my approach? I don't know, but I am eternally grateful for his speed of departure.

October 21, 1986
33 18S 08 56E
Almost midnight. Four hundred and twenty-five miles to go. I am absolutely fed up.

The day has gone from bad to worse. After covering 746 miles in four days at an average speed of 7.7 knots, I have been becalmed for the last two hours. The wind finally quit altogether after a miserable day of light breeze. With the persistent high swell from the northwest we have been rolling uncomfortably, the wind not strong enough to keep the sails filled. Frequent heavy showers of rain add to the general ambience. So close and yet, it seems, so far.

October 22, 1986
33 48S 11 48E
It is 0900 hours. The wind is finally back in force, allowing me to get some sleep. Talked to Mark, who is just a little to the south. He is experiencing much the same weather. It looks as if we will arrive in Cape Town very close to one another. Funny, I feel I know him so well as a friend after our numerous radio conversations, but I cannot put a face to the voice. Saw my first merchant ship today; a very large bulk-carrier, which passed to the south of me on an easterly course.

October 23/86
33 59S 15 00E
Conditions are still very rough. I have sighted several large fishing boats since daybreak, so do not expect to be able to sleep much until arriving in port. Seabirds provide constant companionship now, and porpoises are a common sight. Obviously passing over good fishing grounds! Am hoping to arrive in Cape Town by noon tomorrow, but do not like the sound of the weather forecast. Have a good 40 knots of wind now from the south-south-west, and if it shifts towards the east it will make it very difficult to keep on going.

It is now 1600; I knew it was going to get worse before it got better, but this is just about the last straw. The wind has come around to the south, and the seas are absolutely horrendous. Very steep and breaking, putting a terrible strain on the boat as we try and

47

*beat to windward. The lee rail is continuously under water, and we
are falling off each wave with a terrible crash. Don't know how much
longer Joseph Young—or my nerves—can take it. It seems bloody
unfair, with only one hundred miles to go.*

October 24, 1986
33 52S 17 53E
*Fear for my safety finally overrode my burning desire to make port.
At 0310 this morning the wind became south-easterly, and increased
to a good 50 knots. After several near knockdowns I was forced to
take down the headsail. With any sail up forward of the mast it had
become impossible to keep the bow of the boat into the sea, and taking
one of these breakers on the beam could spell disaster. A bitter pill to
swallow after hearing that Mark arrived at the finish line shortly
after 0600. Table Mountain has been visible since dawn, an incentive
if there ever was one.*

*Heading as close to the wind as I can, the satellite navigator
shows that I am actually crabbing sideways at a speed of four knots.
Fingers crossed, this will put me home free at about six this evening!*

The last few hours of this first leg were as exciting as only a
hard-won landfall can be. It is difficult to describe the feeling of
anticipation as the last few miles slipped by.

The sun was slowly setting behind me as I closed to within
eight miles of the finish. Closer to land, the seas had diminished
slightly, and I was now in constant radio contact with the Race
Committee. The city of Cape Town was spread out before me,
the Seven Apostles and Table Mountain forming a spectacular
backdrop to this most welcome sight. But one more surprise
awaited me. With no warning the wind died completely as I
sailed into the wind shadow of the mountains. Clenching my
fists I screamed in frustration. I dropped down below to speak
on the radio with Robin Knox-Johnston, the Race Chairman. He
assured me that the wind at the line was still blowing hard and
offered encouragement to my lagging spirits.

In 1969, Robin had been the first man ever to complete a non-
stop circumnavigation of the world, alone under sail. As a

youngster I had read and reread his book of the voyage, dreaming that perhaps one day I too would be able to sail the oceans of the world on my own boat. Listening to him now on the radio, knowing that he understood my feelings at that moment, gave me a great boost when I really needed it. I returned to the cockpit.

A few minutes later, unable to stand the wait any longer, I made a big mistake; I hoisted the small #4 jib. No sooner was the sail set, than the wind hit once again, stronger than ever before. Totally out of control, *Joseph Young* literally took off, blasting across the water towards the buoy marking the end of the first leg. Too exhausted to move, I sat with both hands on the tiller, fighting to keep the boat pointing in the right direction. A short half-hour later, careening through the darkness, I saw the lights of several small boats heading rapidly towards me. Within minutes, *Joseph Young* was illuminated by a spotlight as the boats of the National Sea Rescue Institute, acting on behalf of the Race Committee, arrived close alongside.

At last the horn sounded—we had finally completed the first leg! Instantly, *Joseph Young* was boarded by half a dozen rubber-suited figures, who swarmed over the rails in a manner worthy of Errol Flynn. Dazed, I watched as bodies moved in every direction. I had not seen another human being for almost two months and now I was surrounded! Jean-Luc Van Den Heede of *Let's Go* appeared at my side, and forcefully told me to step aside as he grabbed the tiller. A beer was shoved into my hands; my back was pummelled by well-wishers. Very quickly this welcoming crowd had the sails down and a tow connected to take me in to the marina. I had arrived.

From the finish line to the inner harbour was only a short haul, but the weather, if anything, had worsened. With the yacht club wind indicator showing 60 knots it would have been courting disaster to try to manoeuvre the boat into one of the slips at the yacht club. It was decided to secure the boat to an emergency mooring buoy, which was anchored well clear of all obstructions for just such a purpose. After some hair-raising moments, *Joseph Young* was at last safely secured. I grabbed a few essentials, closed the hatch, and tumbled into the little tow boat for the ride ashore. I was amazed to see a small crowd gathered on the outer jetty, one couple proudly holding aloft the Canadian flag. Tears welled in my eyes.

At the marina, another shock awaited me. Literally hundreds of people were standing on the shore singing and clapping to loud music blaring from the clubhouse. My arrival had coincided with the weekly club dance, and the crowd had poured off the dance floor to welcome me in. After having been my own company for so long, I was overwhelmed!

My first steps on solid ground were somewhat shaky, but I soon found my hand gripped by Ian Kiernan, a Class-One entrant, who proffered a bottle of champagne. As I stumbled into the clubhouse, I was confronted by a bearded character whose red-rimmed eyes smiled at me from a face that harboured a look of utter exhaustion. This man looked just the way I felt, but the voice that spoke to me was one that I recognized well.

"Glad to see you made it, John."

A satisfied grin spread across my face. "How the hell are you, Mark?" I replied.

PART TWO

Cape Town to Sydney

My stay in Cape Town lasted for three weeks, just long enough for me to recuperate from the trials of the first leg and to prepare *Joseph Young* for the expected rigours of the second leg.

On my first night ashore, Robin Knox-Johnston and his wife, Susan, were kind enough to drag me away from the yacht club and take me back to the apartment they were staying in. Here, for the first time since Newport, I enjoyed the luxury of a hot bath followed by a huge "breakfast" of fresh eggs, bacon, toast, and tea. The couch upon which I then parked myself for the night seemed to me amazing; not only was it warm and dry, but it was motionless!

As I lay there in the darkness, however, sleep did not come easily. The stillness, the quiet, was overpowering. At sea, I had become attuned to the sounds of the boat in motion. The hissing of water past the hull, inches from my ears as I fell asleep, was an indicator of speed. The faint whirring of the electric motor told me that the self-steering was doing its job. Squeaks and groans from the rigging were separated and identified, marking the strength of the wind on the sails. In sleep, one ear stayed open, the mind unconsciously listening for a change in the pattern.

This first night ashore, I woke several times with a start, only to sink back smiling on the pillows. No need to worry about the next sail change, a gear failure, the wind. I was safe. I could relax.

I rose at a reasonable hour the next morning, anxious to return to the Royal Cape Yacht Club and use the phone installed in the BOC office for the use of the competitors. It had been over two weeks since I had been able to talk to Vicki, and I was dying to hear her voice and let her know that I had arrived safely.

The drive to the club gave me my first glimpse of the city of Cape Town, and it more than lived up to my expectations. Although it was still only early spring, the weather was beautiful; the weather in Cape Town is always beautiful. The mountains behind the city, visible from so far out to sea, were even more spectacular up close. After so long on my own, with only the sounds of the boat, wind, and sea for company, my senses were alive to the noise and bustle of civilization.

At the club, Robin led me straight to the BOC trailer and sat me down with the phone. I felt as nervous as an adolescent on a first date while the connection was being made, and when Vicki answered the phone, an unequalled flood of emotions washed over me. It was as if I suddenly realized that I had actually made it; all the strain of the last two months drained away from me. Hearing her voice without the static and hiss of the radio as a backdrop was a tonic. I was overwhelmingly happy, but I couldn't stop the tears running down my face.

After a conversation that seemed to me far too short, I wandered over to the restaurant where I joined several of the other competitors for breakfast. As the Finnish competitors Pentti Salmi of *Colt by Rettig* and Harry Harkimo of *Belmont Finland*, Hal Roth of *American Flag*, Jean-Luc Van Den Heede of the French boat *Let's Go*, Mark Shrader, and myself sat and chatted, I was struck by the obvious camaraderie that now existed within our group. Although we would hardly have known each other passing in the street, radio contact throughout our shared adventure had knit us closely together. Safely ashore now, we could sit and laugh as we each recounted tales of our hardships during the first leg of the race.

My first priority was to take a good look at *Joseph Young* and assess what work needed to be done. She had taken good care of me during the fifty-five days since we had left Newport; now it was my turn. Arrangements were quickly made with the yard manager, and within the hour *Joseph Young* was secured in a berth right in front of the clubhouse. Since I planned to live on board during my time in Cape Town, I could not have asked for a better spot.

The appearance of my little boat shocked me. First of all, she was quite obviously leaning over to port. A quick inspection revealed that the new gasket I had installed on the leaking cockpit locker had not held up, and the storm of the last few days had completely flooded the space. One more thing to add to the job list I had started while still at sea. Now that I was clean and dry myself, I was appalled at how damp and "lived in" was my little home away from home. I decided to spend the rest of the first day attacking the interior of the boat. Bunk cushions were hung in the rigging to air, and every item of clothing was bagged for a major laundry expedition. I was interrupted in this rather odious task by a retired couple who introduced themselves as Nina and Norman Maclennan, formerly of Montreal, Canada. They had been, they said, the proud wavers of the Canadian flag last night, and were anxious to help me in any way they could. Seeing what I was doing, they insisted on taking my laundry home with them, to be returned the next day sweet-smelling, ironed, and folded. Over the next three weeks Nina and Norman became my unofficial support team, working hard to help me get ready for the next leg of the race. Their kindness to me was unforgettable, and indicative of the spirit that grew throughout the BOC Challenge.

It took a few days to assess thoroughly the condition of *Joseph Young* and to sort out what actually needed to be done before I put back to sea, but overall I was more than pleased with the way she had withstood the rigours of the trip. Several sails needed some minor repair, but the addition of a new Sobstad mainsail to the inventory took care of my major worry. For a small fee, a local diver inspected and cleaned the underwater parts of the boat. He found no apparent problems, so I did not feel the need to have the boat taken out of the water and put on the slip; one thing less to concern myself with. Down below, apart from the mildew, the various bits and pieces were not in bad shape. The generator had been working like clockwork and required only an oil and filter change. The batteries, too, tested well. The satellite navigator, the weather facsimile recorder, and, most important to my enjoyment of life, the cassette deck were all working well. The only item of electronic equipment that had failed, the log, would have to stay that way for the next leg. Pentti Salmi had generously given me some of his spare parts, but it turned out that the fault lay in a unit that I simply could not afford to replace. So, although there were myriad small jobs to attend to, the only major task was the replacement of some rigging.

The failure of the port checkstay just over half way into the first leg had made me a little cautious. To my mind, the problem lay with the type of fitting holding the stay to the mast. There were four similar fittings on the rig, and these I set about replacing. Lars Bergstrom, a member of the support team of *Thursday's Child* (USA), gave me some of his precious time and expertise in designing a proper set of substitutes that I got manufactured locally. Their installation was accomplished with the assistance of Alex, a tireless volunteer with the local race organizers. In his early twenties, Alex seemed to spend all of his spare time helping out at Race Headquarters, working on the various boats when required, and running errands for those of us without vehicles. His assistance, like that of nearly all the volunteers I met during the course of the race, was crucial; without Alex's help, for instance, I'd have had much more difficulty in making the start of the next leg.

All was not work, however; by the third day ashore I had a comfortable routine established that allowed plenty of time for fraternizing with the other competitors. Living on the boat, although it was not my first choice, saved me time in travelling, and gave me a headstart on the day's work. Most mornings I would be awake by seven, and after a shower in the yacht club's facilities, I would punch in a couple of undisturbed hours of work before heading for the restaurant for breakfast. Ten o'clock would find a group of competitors gathered around a table with coffee, hashing out ideas on equipment and tactics, and exchanging information about local suppliers and repair shops. These informal bull sessions were always punctuated with lots of laughter and friendly rivalry.

During our stay in Cape Town, the BOC organizers felt, we ought to get away from the boats now and again and absorb a little of the local atmosphere. To this end they had organized several events and activities. Robin Knox-Johnston, a keen cricket player, had committed the competitors to a match against a team from Afrox, the BOC affiliate in South Africa. He had even been quoted as saying that the BOC Challenge was in fact an international cricket tour in which the players sailed from game to game. The morning of the match, our "team" drove out to the cricket grounds for an hour's intense practice. Here we learned such basics as which way up to hold the bat, how to wear the pads, and what exactly the object of the game was. Needless to say, the match itself was a comic disaster, but it and the other activities achieved the desired objective: our minds were given something to concentrate on besides our boats and the upcoming second leg.

Back at the yacht club the general mood was gradually becoming more subdued as November 15, the day on which the second leg would start, approached. Aboard *Joseph Young*, I was busier than ever as I did those jobs that had to be left till last. Food stores were purchased and carefully stowed away, freshwater tanks flushed and filled, diesel taken on for the generator, and charts for the trip to Sydney laid out and examined. Being tied up directly in front of the clubhouse had proven to be a real advantage. Working away by myself in full view of anyone inside, I had more offers of help from club members than I knew what to do with. One gentleman (whose name, alas, I forget) approached me one morning as I was replacing the lashings on the dodger, the canopy that protects the main hatch from spray and wind. He was aghast that I actually planned to sail down to the cold southern oceans with such meagre protection. He explained that he owned a company that specialized in making dodgers, and insisted on taking mine away for modification. It was returned much improved the very next day, free of charge. Such was the atmosphere around the marina.

Two days left before the start. All the boats had passed the Race Committee's safety inspection. Adrenalin was starting to flow; the laughs were a little tighter now. Nineteen of us, survivors of the twenty-five who had started the race in Newport, filed in to the skipper's briefing that morning. No longer with us were *Quailo*, now safely arrived in Rio de Janeiro; *Airforce*, sunk after colliding with debris in the water; *Madonna*, retired with rigging damage; *Neptune's Express*, dismasted; ACI *Crusader*, whose skipper had been injured; and *Miss Global*, retired to Rio de Janeiro after losing her rudder.

The purpose of the briefing was to provide us with all pertinent information regarding the sailing of the next leg. Procedures for the start were discussed, radio frequencies and times for daily chat hours laid down, particular navigational hazards noted, and the latest weather information passed out. I was shocked when the discussion turned to icebergs. That icebergs inhabited the southern oceans was common knowledge, but normally they were confined to latitudes below approximately 50 degrees south. Unconfirmed reports, we were told, spoke of ice sightings as far north as 43 degrees south. No further information was available. For those of us without radar, this posed a grave hazard, and gave us good reason to reconsider our planned routes. In brief, the farther south one sailed on a course between Africa and Australia, the shorter the distance but the greater the risk of running into icebergs. If one looks at a globe, in fact, it's clear that the most direct route between the two ports is directly across Antarctica. We would each have to weigh the risks, and decide for ourselves what constituted a fair balance between speed and safety.

Saturday, the morning of the start. I rose slightly earlier than usual and hurried off for my morning shower. I lingered a little longer under the stream of hot water, acutely aware that it would be forty days or more before I could again enjoy such a luxury. But finally, clean and dressed, I returned to *Joseph Young* and put on a pot of coffee. The prize-giving ceremonies for the first leg had been held the evening before, a gala event that had left me with a real need for strong morning coffee. Sitting down at the chart table, I wrote a last letter to Vicki, urging her to consider meeting me in Australia. I needed that incentive to keep me going.

The weather that morning was fine and clear, despite a forecast calling for gale-force winds by nightfall. As the other competitors started arriving at the club, I joined them for our last breakfast together. There was a lot of bravado being displayed over the meal, but I hoped that they were feeling as nervous as I. By the time that we got up from the table, the breeze had freshened considerably, perhaps a little foretaste of what was to come.

After breakfast I walked over to the BOC office to make my last call home. Except for the secretary, I was glad to see the trailer was empty. I thought I might need the privacy and I did. Talking to Vicki I tried hard to remain strong and confident, but emotion got the upper hand. By the time I hung up the phone, the secretary on the other side of the desk was crying harder than I was. The sooner I was away now, the better.

With only seconds to go, I hardened up on the sheets and headed towards the line. A loud bang and a puff of smoke from the starting gun signalled the start of the second leg. We were away! The breeze was stiff, and under a double-reefed mainsail and #4 jib *Joseph Young* was moving well, crossing the line sixth. What happened next was almost funny. As each of us sailed into the wind shadow of the mountains, the wind dropped away to literally nothing. Within minutes the entire fleet was left drifting along with our sails set for a good breeze! A mad scramble ensued as we each raced to hoist more sail. For once, having a small boat was an advantage, and within ten minutes *Joseph Young* was creeping along, the drifter catching the occasional puffs of wind that wafted across the water. Feeling like King for a Day, I nursed the helm as we ghosted past first one, then another of the larger, heavier yachts. Inshore, I could see one competitor struggling to keep his spinnaker filled, and resolved to angle away from the coast slightly in hopes of finding a bit more breeze. Astern of me the rest of the fleet gradually became indistinguishable from one another and then were lost from view. I soon felt as if I were alone upon the sea once again. As the afternoon waned several helicopters out for pictures buzzed me, but other than that it was a beautifully quiet sail, the rugged coast of South Africa off to port leading the way southward. Not particularly wanting to cook a proper supper the first night out, I contented myself with chewing on strips of biltong, or dried meat, carved from the leg of lamb hanging below, a gift from the Rotary Club in Cape Town. It was surprisingly good washed down with a cup of tea, and would last me well into the voyage.

Three hours later conditions had again changed dramatically. With the onset of darkness the wind had piped up, and we were starting to make heavy going of it as we pounded to windward under a single reef and the #3 headsail. It looked, for once, as if the forecast was coming true, and I expected a full gale from the south-east before the night was out. I hoped to pass the Cape of Good Hope before midnight, and planned to stay to the west of the Agulhas Bank. This area of shallower water stretching south from the African continent is known for its nasty seas during a blow; the sooner I got south of it the better. I kept as good a look-out as possible in the worsening weather. This close to the shore one could expect fishing boats and coastal shipping. I also didn't fancy the idea of being run down by a sixty-foot yacht passing me from astern!

By 2200 hours the weather had deteriorated to the point of absolute misery. Even with minimum sail up, the punishment was extreme. *Joseph Young* pushed bravely into the breaking seas, but with every fifth or sixth swell crashing solidly across the deck, it was only a matter of time before I would have to heave to. Bruised and battered by the violent motion of the boat, and not having yet aquired my ''sea legs,'' I was demoralized to think of the 6,500 miles between here and the next stopover. What a lousy way to start out!

Soaking wet, cold, tired, and scared, I slid back the hatch and started below for a mug of something hot. At that moment the boat lurched and I tumbled down to land heavily on my knees. As I struggled back to my feet something inside me seemed to let go and my fear metamorphosed into anger. Throwing back my head, I screamed obscenities, cursing the wind, the ocean, the rain, the boat, and my own stupidity for being out here in the first place. Feeling a little better after my outburst, I put some water on to boil, and wedged myself in a corner to calm down . . . I wondered how the rest of the guys were making out.

As I sipped gratefully on my hot coffee, I concluded that if there was no improvement within the half-hour I would shorten sail. The noise down in the cabin as we thrashed southwards was tremendous, and it set my nerves on edge. Never mind the boat, I wasn't sure how much more of this *I* could take!

All of a sudden, I heard a strange scream and a shudder reverberated through the hull. Choking on a mouthful of coffee, I sensed real trouble. I grabbed the spotlight and leapt out on deck. The rain and spray sweeping across the boat in the darkness made it hard to see properly, but a quick check of the deck revealed nothing. Shining the light upwards, I scanned the mast. What I saw made my stomach churn! About halfway up the mast, between the upper and lower spreaders, the rig had taken a gross bend off to starboard and was flexing badly with every wave. Really frightened now, I scrambled to cast off the main halyard. Clawing my way along the deck, I braced myself against the boom and frantically dragged at the mainsail, desperate to reduce the pressure on the mast. A wave broke over the deck and knocked my feet from under me. Cursing, I clung to the boom and regained my balance. At last the sail was down and lashed. Dry-mouthed, chest heaving, I struggled back to the relative safety of the cockpit to retrieve the spotlight for a closer inspection. Once again I set off forward, crabbing along the deck on hands and knees until I could wrap an arm around the mast. Peering into the blackness, I could discern no visible sign of a failure: the rigging appeared to be intact: the chainplates showed no sign of strain. I couldn't understand what was happening, but knew that my choices were few: I could carry on, hoping that the weather would ease before the mast broke, and that I could fix whatever it was that had let go, or I could to turn back for Cape Town and carry out repairs in the safety of the harbour. I agonized over the decision for about twenty minutes before common sense carried the moment. Reluctantly, I put the helm down and turned *Joseph Young* around. I felt like a real loser.

With the wind and sea behind us, the motion was much more comfortable, and our speed almost doubled. According to the chart, we were only about thirty-five miles from Cape Town. I tried to be optimistic — it was possible that I could be back at the marina before breakfast. The extent of the problem was still unknown, of course, but if it was not too serious there was every chance that I could be underway again before nightfall. The worst scenario did not bear thinking about.

My next concern was to inform the Race Committee of my predicament and my estimated time of arrival. Because I had no engine on the boat, it was essential that I arrange a tow back in to the yacht club. Fortunately, Cape Town Radio was quick in making the connection for me, and I was immediately put through to BOC, where volunteers still standing by informed that a welcoming committee would be on hand for my arrival. Much reassured, I returned to the deck and the business at hand. It was going to be a long night.

The morning sun rose on *Joseph Young* a scant eight miles from the harbour breakwater. The wind had disappeared almost completely with the coming of dawn, and, as I was afraid to raise too much sail with safety so close at hand, we were ghosting along on an almost flat sea. Rather than simply cross yesterday's start line going the other way, I was required by a ruling from the local organizers to enter the outer harbour unaided. This added a nail-biting two miles to the return journey, watching precious minutes tick by, and I was much relieved when a tow line was finally tossed over from the Committee boat. A few minutes later, welcoming hands reached out to offer assistance as we slipped into the berth. Looking aloft to the mast, still in one piece, I counted my blessings and wondered how many of my nine lives I had used up!

I was overwhelmed by the number of friends who had turned up to help me. A quick trip up the mast revealed no outward sign of what had caused the mast to bend, so I explained the events of the previous evening to Lars Bergstrom, the *Thursday's Child* support member who had been so much help to me over the past few weeks. He assured me that he and the others would thoroughly check things over and take care of the repairs, and he urged me ashore for some breakfast; with Nina and Norman Maclennan taking me firmly in tow I could hardly resist! After eighteen exhausting hours at sea without proper food or sleep, finding myself sitting in front of a real breakfast was an undeniable pleasure, and I wolfed it down.

After the meal I returned to the boat to find that my impromptu pit crew had found the source of the trouble to be a couple of failed turnbuckles. They refused to allow me to help, insisting that the best thing I could do was to go and get some sleep. Once again, Norman and Nina came to the rescue and offered me a berth on their yacht, just across the marina. Within five minutes of crawling into the bunk I was sound asleep with Nina standing guard to ensure that I was not disturbed.

Five hours later I woke up, startled momentarily to find myself in strange surroundings. Someone was calling me from the galley. Groaning, I struggled into my clothes and emerged from the cabin to be met by a welcome mug of coffee proffered by Norman. It was four o'clock in the afternoon. Over a quick bite to eat, Norman informed me that *Joseph Young* was ready to go, and gave me some other good news. It seemed that the wind, which had so cruelly left me earlier this morning, had done the same to the rest of the fleet. The bulk of them were sitting just south of the Cape of Good Hope in drifting conditions, while here in Cape Town a light breeze still persisted. Perhaps I would be given a chance to catch up. Tempering this was a report that another competitor had turned back, and that the gale had caused damage to several other boats. Although it was hard not to be happy with the weather report, I certainly didn't wish bad luck on the others, and hoped that none of them was having serious problems.

Perhaps it was memories of the previous night, or perhaps the lack of peer pressure without the organized start and the presence of the other sailors, but I felt a distinct reluctance to head back out to sea. Good-byes to my small band of helpers and well-wishers were prolonged, but eventually I could delay no longer. Stepping aboard and casting off the lines I was eased out of the slip by the yacht club's tender. Twenty-seven hours after yesterday's send-off, *Joseph Young* and I quietly slipped out of Cape Town harbour for the last time.

Two hours later I was feeling very much better. Although the wind was light, it was enough to keep *Joseph Young* moving steadily over the mirror-like sea. I couldn't help but enjoy an evening this beautiful. Except for the gentle gurgle of water sliding past the hull it was completely quiet. With each passing mile my confidence built, and I resolved to do my utmost to catch up with the pack. My thoughts turned to Vicki and home.

I had been unable to bring myself to phone her while I was back in port, though I had wanted to very badly. I wondered now whether that had been the right decision, but saying a long-distance good-bye had been so hard the first time that I didn't want to put either of us through it again so soon. Perhaps I would be able to get a radio call through in a week or so when my mood was a little more upbeat, and I could pass along good news, not bad.

I sat up in the bunk with a start, banging my head so hard on the overhanging shelf that I almost went back down for the count. One hand on my skull, I was wondering what had interrupted my nap so violently when the VHF radio gave me the answer. I had turned the volume up full when I lay down for an hour's snooze, in case an approaching ship should try to make contact. Now Cape Town Radio was calling me on channel 16. Picking up the microphone I responded, to be told that a telephone link awaited me on a working channel. Puzzled—and a little alarmed—I switched frequencies. Much to my surprise it was Eric, one of the stalwarts who had given me so much help in port, phoning to make sure everything was still going well and to wish me a final bon voyage. I was really touched by his concern; it seemed to encapsulate the incredible kindness shown to me by everybody in Cape Town. The spirit of shared adventure generated by this race was truly wonderful.

The middle stretch of the night, though sleepless, passed without incident. Trying to get the best out of the boat I spent long periods at the helm. Shortly before the first light of dawn I clambered down below to brew a pot of tea and to check my progress with the position on the satellite navigator. To my absolute horror, I found that the display screen on the satellite navigator had gone blank! A quick check, however, revealed that the problem was only a loose fuse holder, and within a few minutes this piece of electronic wizardry was back on the job. Without it, I would have had to fall back on the sun and stars for navigation, not in itself a problem except for the frequency of complete cloud cover in these latitudes. I went back to my pot of tea and followed that with a short sleep. It was almost light outside now, and we were sailing on a southerly course just clear of the Cape of Good Hope and the shipping lanes. It finally seemed like I was really on my way.

For months, years even, I had been anticipating this portion of the voyage with both excitement and fear. Tales told by others who had brought their small boats across the southern oceans spoke of incessant gale-force winds from the west; of swells and waves surging around the world, growing to immense proportions without any land mass to interrupt their passage, urged on by the wind and current. After the first week, I was becoming a skeptic.

As each day passed *Joseph Young* and I were edging farther and farther south, ever closer to the infamous "Roaring Forties." With every sunrise I waited for the beginning of the westerly gales, always in vain. My log-book tells of long nights with violent squalls, heavy rain showers, and much lightning, but, although the wind direction was forever shifting, rarely did it blow from the west.

November 19, 1986
37 33S 24 03W
Wind south-south-east at Force 5. Three reefs in main and #3. Close-hauled on starboard tack. So much for a sleigh ride!

November 20, 1986
37 39S 26 20E
Absolutely miserable. Heavy south-easterly sea and cross swell. Pounding heavily. Motion terrible, very wet. Wondering what we're trying to prove and to whom.

Sea and bird life was in great evidence during that first week, always a welcome sight, though sometimes a bit close for my liking. About mid-morning on November 17, I was at the helm, keeping a good eye on the surrounding water. There had been numerous whales visible earlier, and I was anxious not to intrude upon their space. Out of the corner of my eye I suddenly noticed a disturbance in the water. Turning quickly I was stunned to see not a whale, but a large, white-bellied shark slide by. My low opinion of swimming as a recreational pastime was reinforced. Arriving on deck at seven in the morning two days later, I was surprised to find an unwelcome passenger in the cockpit—a jellyfish. It must have been washed aboard by a wave during the night. Wary of being stung, I donned a pair of heavy rubber gloves before picking it up and dropping it over the side.

On November 22, the wind was from the north and *Joseph Young* was going along nicely with the self-steering keeping the course. Just after lunch I was sitting on deck enjoying the reprieve in the weather when I saw, a mere hundred yards off the port quarter, a large whale heading straight towards me. Terrified, I leapt for the tiller and disconnected the auto-pilot. Shoving the helm hard over I did a quick ninety-degree turn to port, heading almost straight into the wind. Eyes glued on the whale, I watched dry-mouthed as it charged through the boat's wake, missing us by no more than fifteen feet! Badly shaken, I reset the course and quickly trimmed the sails, willing *Joseph Young* back up to speed. The beast had disappeared, but I feared a repeat performance. Whether the whale had intended to hit me or more likely simply hadn't seen me, I had no way of knowing, but I certainly didn't want to hang about and test any theories!

The next afternoon I at last felt like I was "back in the running." The fleet positions no longer had me in last place, which gave my spirits a boost. The weather, however, had taken a strange turn. Under the influence of an unusually large high-pressure system, which had moved down from the north, the westerly winds had been pushed far to the south. For all of us caught in this trap, the next several days would yield light and fickle winds. This, as it turned out, was to be the calm before the storm.

Being becalmed gave me the opportunity to do some much-needed maintenance on the boat. During an earlier squall a shackle had parted on one of the checkstays, so I changed both of them for a more suitable fitting. All the standing rigging was looked over carefully, and I tightened several of the shrouds a little. With the tape deck blasting out a selection of Joe Cocker and Elton John tunes, the morning passed quickly. The elation I felt at still being in the game, and not stuck back in Cape Town with major rigging problems is difficult to describe, but it was as if a major hurdle had been jumped. Christmas in Australia was my next goal.

After lunch I settled down to play electrician. Once again the satellite navigator was giving trouble; it had not calculated a fix since eight o'clock that morning. Removing it from its mountings, I laid it out on the chart table and carefully unscrewed the cover plates. I was hoping that a loose connection would show itself as the cause of the problem; anything more complicated would be beyond my limited talents. Alas, I found no obvious fault, so I reassembled the unit and turned it on. Not surprisingly, it didn't work. I dug out my sextant and polished the mirrors. It looked like I was going to have to find Sydney harbour without the aid of modern technology.

With time on our hands, the daily chat sessions between boats were becoming longer and longer, providing some good entertainment. Friendships had been cemented during our stopover in Cape Town, and the conversations were a lot less serious as a result. Bertie Reed, the well-known South African sailing *Stabilo Boss*, became the official organizer of a sort of in-house lottery. The wager was ten dollars Australian, and we all passed along our best estimated time of arrival at the finish line in Sydney. Whoever arrived closest to their time would collect the pot. I bet on three in the morning, December 28; as it turned out, I was glad to lose — I overestimated my time by three days.

A report on the positions of all the yachts in the race,

obtained from the Argos transmitters carried on board, was being broadcast to the fleet at noon every day by Alistair Campbell, a South African ham-radio operator. While copying down the positions on November 25 I was astonished to see that the American *Thursday's Child*, sailed by Warren Luhrs, was almost on top of me. Dashing up on deck, I could hardly believe my eyes. There, off to the west-north-west, was a sail on the horizon. It had to be Warren! This unintentional rendezvous with a fellow competitor, a friend, over 1,200 miles out to sea was a fantastic moment. Back down below, I switched on the VHF radio and put out a call. I was not really surprised when Warren's voice came back to me almost immediately. He, too, had obviously taken note of the Argos positions. *Thursday's Child* had also been forced back to Cape Town that first night and I inquired about the problems that he had had. Apparently everything had been repaired in short order, but Warren's disappointment was evident. He had probably the fastest boat in the race, but after having had to restart both the first and the second legs, he had a lot of catching up to do. Luck was definitely not on his side. After wishing each other fair winds and a safe trip we signed off the air. I hurried back on deck to watch this fleeting contact with another human being fade over the horizon.

After supper that evening I sat down at the chart table to write a letter to Vicki, only my second since leaving Cape Town. Less than a quarter of the way into the second leg my thoughts were already on the Sydney stopover; would I be spending Christmas alone at sea, or on shore in Sydney with Vicki? I was desperate to receive the news that she would be coming Down Under, afraid to hear that she would not. All I could do was wait and hope. I knew beyond a shadow of a doubt that separation was harder on the ones left behind than on me. I had the satisfaction of reaching for a long-dreamt of goal. My fears were of things tangible; Vicki's and my family's were of the unknown, of what news the next phone call might bring.

A few hours after dark the wind started to blow from the north-west, a little foretaste of a southern-ocean gale. The barometer had been falling all day, slowly but steadily, as the high-pressure system moved off to the east. By midnight *Joseph Young* was going along at over 8 knots, one reef tucked in the mainsail. The sea was building, but as we were now on an almost easterly course, it was coming from almost astern and was not making life too unpleasant. Before the wind had filled in, Mark Schrader on *Lone Star* had been a little to the south of me and farther west. I had found I liked having somebody behind me, and I was determined to try and keep it that way. Accordingly, I sailed hard through the night, and at noon the next day had logged 195 miles in twenty-four hours. Imagine my disappointment when the Argos report showed Mark had crept a little closer. The wind eased a little in the afternoon so I wasted no time in cranking up some more sail.

Although the seas were down a little from yesterday, there was a new factor in the weather that kept my nerves on edge — fog. Coming hand-in-hand with the drop in temperature, the fog had reduced visibility to less than four hundred yards and romping along at well over 8 knots left one little time to take avoiding action if it became necessary. Without radar, I relied entirely on sight and sound to warn me of any obstacles that might lie ahead and my recent encounters with whales, as well as the ever-increasing possibility of encountering icebergs, made it hard to relax. Still, the odds were in my favour, and I knew Mark would be going all out to pass me.

The noon position on November 27 showed another twenty-four-hour run of 195 miles. This time I had held Mark at bay, and I jokingly chided him on the evening chat hour for slacking off. Feeling quite content with the way *Joseph Young* was performing I turned in for a nap at about ten o'clock.

I wakened at midnight sensing a definite change in the rhythm of the boat's motion. Lying there for a moment, loath to leave the damp warmth of the sleeping bag, I listened. The noise of the wind in the rigging had become a muffled shriek, the sound of the sea against the hull was like a waterfall. I struggled from the bunk and reluctantly pulled on a heavy sweater and wet, clammy oilskins. I slid open the hatch, allowing a cold wind to blast straight into the cabin—a full gale was now blowing from the north-west. In the darkness I could see flashes of white as the crests of the waves broke and tumbled, lines of spume streaking off downwind. *Joseph Young* was rocketing ahead of the sea, grossly over-canvassed. Pulling myself up on deck, I clipped on the safety harness and scrambled forward on my hands and knees to take down the headsail. With the foredeck virtually awash, my fingers were soon numbed by the cold water, dulling the sting of salt finding its way into every cut and blister. I talked myself through the whole procedure, packing the #2 away in the bag, which was then shoved down the forehatch (along with several gallons of water), and dragging the #4 jib, a small, heavy sail, up on deck, to reverse the process. Then it was back to the cockpit to winch away on the halyard and trim the sheet until the jib was drawing properly. After a short pause for breath, I worked myself forward again to tuck a third reef in the mainsail. Working away by the mast, I sang loudly to be heard above the noise of the gale, stopping now and again to curse a particularily mean-looking wave as it reared up astern. Finally, after about forty minutes of hard labour, everything was in order, and I retreated to the relative warmth of the cabin and the comfort of a hot mug of cocoa. If conditions didn't deteriorate any further within the hour, I'd try for another sleep.

Once more, for the third day running, my position at noon posted a run of 195 miles over the last twenty-four hours for an average speed of 8.1 knots. Mark was still hot on my tail despite my best efforts to increase the lead. At seven that evening the gale finally blew itself out, the wind shifting to the south-west, and dropped to a sedate Force 3. Although the breeze persisted through the night, the following afternoon found me virtually becalmed once again, the sails slatting horribly in the large swell.

That morning, I had spoken with Mark on the VHF radio, a set that had a range of only about thirty-odd miles. We were now very close. We were even talking about the possibility of actually sighting each other, and agreed to a photo shoot if the

71

occasion should arise. I tried hard not to let the lack of wind discourage me; weather maps from South Africa showed a strong cold front moving our way, a sure sign of more gale-force winds!

Harry Mitchell, the Englishman in the race and at sixty-two the "old man of the sea" among us, sounded absolutely exhausted on the radio this evening. He too had experienced last night's gale, and at one point had been thrown bodily across his cabin by a violent wave. He feared that he had broken a few of his ribs and was in much pain despite strapping his chest. Listening to him I had to chuckle, not at his misfortune, but at his description of the event. The use of the adjective *diabolical* had become Harry's trademark on the chat hour, and he used it unsparingly now in his account of the accident. As to how he was to cope with the injury, his approach was, and had to be, very pragmatic. "Well," he said, "there's not much anyone can do for me out here, is there? I'll just have to press on."

Before the week was out, Harry's injury was to bring him more trouble than he'd bargained for.

One opportunity that this brief period of calm weather brought me was a chance to work on repairs to the satellite navigator. Alistair Campbell, the ham-radio operator who was keeping us up to date on each other's positions, had passed along some advice from an electronics professional, and I set about following his instructions. The cure, I was told, would be to supply a nine-volt current from an external source to the antenna amplifier. Great, but the boat's power supply was all twelve volts! No problem, I said to myself, all I need is a three-volt drop in the circuit before it gets to the amplifier. On board, I had several spare flashlights (all three-volt) so, using parts from two of them, I built a simple little circuit, wired it up to the main switchboard, and spliced the whole lot into the co-axial cable leading up to the antenna. The job took several hours to complete, but when I turned the machine on, much to my amazement it worked! It certainly wasn't perfect, giving me only one, sometimes two, positions a day. Still, it gave me great peace of mind to know that I would have some help in navigating the Bass Straits towards the end of this leg. That night I celebrated with a good stiff hot rum toddy!

December 2, 1986
45 33S 67 06E

Just over three weeks to Christmas. We are back in full gale conditions, with an absolutely incredible sea running. For the first time, the sheer size of the waves, looming up astern as big as apartment buildings, has got me frightened. Joseph Young *is handling it very well, but I feel so insignificant, so small, in the face of such immense power. Thinking about the potential for disaster makes it impossible to relax and I have spent hours at the helm nursing my little boat along. I managed a few hours' sleep earlier this morning, lying on the cabin floor, fully dressed in foul-weather gear and safety harness. I do not feel very confident, wondering if I have finally bitten off more than I can chew.*

At four in the afternoon I switched over control of the boat to the automatic steering and struggled down below. The noise of the wind and sea is terrific in the cabin, but not having to watch the heaving ocean eases the tension a little. A bit like sticking one's head in the sand! Brewing a quick mug of instant soup, I stand by on the radio for the chat hour and news of the other yachts.

Before long the radio crackles to life as the competitors call in. The conditions are the same for all of us at the back of the pack, it seems, and word of the severe gale is passed on to the front runners. Talking to Mark, he is still very close, though edging a bit farther south than me despite the weather. This contact with friends, and knowing that I am not the only one out here, helps tremendously in putting on a brave face. Hal Roth on American Flag *and Mark are deep in conversation when Pentti Salmi aboard* Colt by Rettig *cuts in with an urgent message. My stomach churns; surely things cannot get worse. I listen, aghast, as Pentti reports sighting a large iceberg a short while ago, just to the north of his track. What's more, he can offer only an approximate position for it—his satellite navigator has broken down too. To further complicate matters, I am* not entirely sure of my own position. The crude repair job performed on Joseph Youngs' satellite navigator has not yielded a position fix for eighteen hours. During that time we have travelled over 150 miles; a weak current or a small error on the compass could easily throw out my estimated position by ten or more miles. Fighting down a creeping panic, I lurch over to the chart table and shakily plot the rough positions of the iceberg and myself. The margin for error is slim. According to the information I have, the iceberg is forty miles ahead of me, and about ten miles to the north. There are too many unanswerable questions. How fast and in what direction is the berg drifting? What about growlers, house-sized pieces of ice that break off the main berg? And if one iceberg, why not a whole string of them? The odds do not seem to be in my favour.

Poking my head up through the hatch for a quick look around, I simply cannot believe it. On top of everything else, a heavy, wet fog has rolled in, so thick that I can barely see the bow of the boat, only thirty feet away. My chances of seeing an iceberg on a clear night with a heavy sea running were next to nil, now they are absolutely zero. It will be dark soon, and at least six hours must pass before I am past the danger area. I suddenly feel very tired.

Back on the radio, I agree with Mark to maintain an hourly radio contact throughout the night. It seems that there is really very little I can do to lessen the risk. Heaving to, stopping the boat, is, in my opinion, simply too dangerous in these sea conditions. I could alter course slightly and still keep the waves on my stern, but to what purpose? For all I know, that would only put me on a collision course with the iceberg. I might as well keep going as I am and trust to luck. Not exactly reassuring. For the first — and only — time of the voyage, I pull on my survival suit, and the long vigil in the cockpit begins.

The time passes slowly, broken only by the brief hourly communications with Lone Star. The sailing is eerie in the extreme. In the darkness the only light is the dim red glow shed by the compass. Rocketing along in the fog, surfing down the faces of unseen waves, I have a strange sense of being stationary. Looking along the deck, I see nothing that might indicate movement; I feel as though I am hanging in a cloud. Every once in a while I look down

*at the water directly alongside the hull to orientate myself. Once a
sudden streak of phosphorescence in the sea made me start. Peering
into the blackness I realized that I was being raced by a group of
porpoises. Beautiful to watch, they darted and wove beside* Joseph
Young *for an hour or more.*

By eleven o'clock that night I had passed the reported position
of the iceberg without so much as a sign of its presence, but it
took me a further few hours to unwind sufficiently to be able to
sleep, once again on the cabin floor, wedged in place by spare
lifejackets. Outside, the gale raged unabated. At nine the following morning I received the first satellite fix in forty-six hours.
I was some twenty-three miles to the north of my estimated
position. How close I passed to the iceberg I will never (and
perhaps would rather not) know.

That same afternoon the radio chat hour sounded like a war
report as boat after boat called in with tales of storm damage.
Belmont Finland had been knocked flat by a wave, and Harry
Harkimo had been swept overboard, saved only by his safety
harness. *Stabilo Boss* had suffered the same fate and Bertie Reed
had lost all electrical power after his generator was torn from its
mounts.(He had also gashed his arm, which later became
infected, forcing him to head for Albany, Australia, to receive
medical attention.) Mike Plant aboard *Airco Distributor* also
reported being knocked down but had emerged relatively
unscathed. Richard Konkolski on *Declaration of Independence* told
of breaking a spinnaker pole in a bad broach. *Skoiern IV*, Jacques
de Roux's rocketship, had perhaps suffered the most, having
being rolled over twice. His masthead instruments and satellite-
navigation antenna had been swept away, and his steering
wheel had been damaged to the point of unusability. Although
he was able to control the boat with the emergency tiller, Jacques
would have a hard time of it for the remainder of the leg. Of the
greatest concern was the silence of Harry Mitchell aboard *Double
Cross*. He had not been heard from for almost twenty-four
hours. When his voice finally cut through the airwaves near the
end of the chat hour, my heart soared with relief. His news,

however, was not good. It seems Harry had blacked out completely sometime during the early morning, possibly from the pain of knocking his already-broken ribs. He had come to almost eight hours later, lying on the cabin floor in a pool of dried blood. Able at first to open only one eye, he had feared the worst, but was relieved to find that the other was just sealed by clotted blood. In great pain, ribs cracked, a bad gash over one eye, and probably concussed, Harry received medical advice from shore via the radio, and decided to carry on. I took my hat off to him.

When this vicious gale finally eased on December 4, *Joseph Young* had logged 843 miles in four days—an average speed of 8.8 knots. We were almost at the halfway point for this second leg, and I was starting to feel optimistic about my chances of reaching Sydney in time for Christmas. There were still, however, over 3,000 miles of ocean to cross before reaching port. That the next three weeks would be tough, I had no doubt. What I did not envision was the tragedy that lay just around the corner.

The brief respite from gales at the end of December's first week afforded me an opportunity to make a phone call home to Vicki. I had tried several times over the previous few days, but the weather had played havoc with the radio reception. To finally get through with a clear line, bringing her voice down into the tiny cabin so many miles from home, was an unequalled morale booster. After the fear and hardship of my first real southern-ocean gale, I needed to share my relief and satisfaction at having come through unscathed. After assuring each other that we were doing just fine, we chatted of smaller things, me hanging on every word. After the call, as always, I was left with a happy ache, euphoric over the brief contact, saddened by the distance between us.

On the afternoon of December 8 the wind started to blow hard again from the west. Two brief periods of calm during the preceding forty-eight hours had proved very frustrating, and had allowed Mark, who was following an easterly track just a little farther to the south than my own, to slip by me. My only consolation was that broken cloud had given me a chance to hang my sodden sleeping bag in the rigging for a few hours, and to open up the boat to air out. It felt good, now that I had to batten down again with the onset of more bad weather, to have been able to freshen up a bit. At noon on December 8 I showed a day's run of 219 miles, so the speed was back up. So too was the sea, and conditions were made more uncomfortable by a high cross swell from the north. Careening down the waves and lurching up and over the swell became exhausting. Even the simplest of tasks required twice as much physical effort to carry out. Simply standing still seemed to be no mean feat. Fatigue dulled my mind; that is my only excuse for doing some-thing that night that was unbelievably stupid and that could have proved fatal.

Before turning in to try and snatch a little sleep, I had made myself a hot rum toddy. In the colder temperatures of the second leg, this had become a little ritual, something to brace me for the shock of a cold, damp bunk. The hatch was tightly sealed against the weather, muffling the sound of the elements to a dull roar. Legs wedged against the workbench, I sat on the settee, sipping at my scalding mug of spiced rum and honey. Something suddenly told me that I should be charging the batteries, so without a second thought I grappled my way aft and fired up the diesel generator. I then resumed my position on the settee. After nursing my drink for about five minutes I started to feel a little light-headed. This rum was obviously pretty potent stuff. Through a thickening mental fog, I registered an increase in the wind outside. Air was whistling past the tight rubber seal around the mast, where it passed through the deck from its seat on the keel. The noise was like the whistle on a kettle, and it was starting to get on my nerves. Swallowing the last of the toddy, I pulled myself upright to go and check out this latest annoyance. I staggered and almost fell. Drunk after one weak pick-me-up — unbelievable! Blinking hard, I stared blearily at the main hatch. What I needed was a breath of fresh air. Moving slowly, using both hands to steady myself, I crept aft again. Standing under the hatch, I wrapped one arm around the companionway ladder for support, and with the other reached up and snapped back the four latches holding it closed. In order to slide the hatch open, it was first necessary to raise it a quarter of an inch. Pushing against it with my free hand I couldn't budge it at all. Dizzy, gasping for breath, I let go of the ladder and slammed both palms hard upwards. The hatch yielded with a sucking sound and a violent inrush of fresh air, making my eardrums pop with the change in pressure. Clambering up, I lay half out of the companionway, chest heaving and close to vomiting. The realization of what I had done slowly came to me. The generator had burned up almost all the oxygen in the virtually airtight cabin. The whistling around the mast was caused by a vacuum forming down below. I had been stupid, and very, very, lucky. I mentally put a big X through another of my nine lives.

This second gale that blew through the fleet was more intense even than the first, though of much shorter duration.

For me, it peaked at three in the morning on December 10, when a large wave breaking over the deck woke me from a less than deep sleep. On deck, the wind was gusting at over 50 knots, and the strain on the boat forced me to take down the mainsail entirely. After a brief, adrenalin-pumping struggle, the sail was lashed and stowed on the boom. Although this made the boat more manageable, and therefore safer, it also made the ride more uncomfortable. Without the steadying effect of the main-sail, *Joseph Young* rolled heavily in the following sea. I stayed on deck now, hand steering through the worst of it. By seven, the barometer had started to rise, and with the passing of the front the wind shifted to the south-west and dropped to a moderate Force 5. I gybed, and set about hoisting the main once again. As always, after coming through a hard gale, it took a great deal of mental determination for me to put up more sail area. The temp-tation to relax and be content with plodding along safely and slowly for a while was almost overpowering. With no one watching to goad me into action, it was easy to rationalize; per-haps this is just a temporary lull, the wind will probably pick up again soon, let's give it a few hours and see what happens. I had to remind myself that with the Argos tracking beacon on board, people ashore were, in essence, watching my move-ments, and that however uneven a contest, this was a *race*. I held sometimes lengthy internal debates, taunting my weaker self until pride forced me to take firm control and get moving again.

December 10, 1986
45 04S 99 26E
The importance of radio contact with the other competitors in dispelling feelings of loneliness and isolation was brought home to me yesterday in a big way. Tuning in for the chat hour, I listened to a few of the guys mulling over last night's weather. When the conversation finished, Mark called me up in the usual fashion. Keying the microphone to reply, I was shocked to see that the transmit light on the radio did not light up. Mark called me a second time. Becoming frantic, I repeatedly jammed in the mike key, to no

avail. I listened as Mark then called Hal Roth and asked him to try me. "American Flag calling Joseph Young. Are you there, John?" came the call. Try as I might, banging the microphone now, and jiggling the connections, my radio refused to transmit. Beside myself with helplessness I heard Mark and Hal discussing my silence. Never before had I missed a radio schedule. Mark was obviously worried, which touched me. The feeling I had was very strange; I was a prisoner behind a two-way mirror, desperately wanting to join the activity in the room, but unable to be seen or heard. Repairing the radio before the next chat hour became of paramount importance to me.

By the afternoon the seas had smoothed out enough to enable work on the radio to begin without risk of my damaging it further by dropping or banging it due to the motion of the boat. Disassembling the microphone, I found no evidence of anything out of order. Checking the connections to and from the radio itself revealed no faults either. The next step was to unbolt the set from its mountings, and remove the cover. Looking into the inner workings of the radio, I could see no obvious loose wires or damaged components. I sat down with the service manual for a while, then traced back the wires leading from the radio to the antenna coupler, installed in the stern of the boat. These wires all incorporated in-line fuse holders, and it was here that I found what I hoped was the problem. Moisture had attacked one of them, building up a crust of corrosion. After giving it a good clean, I reassembled the whole works and switched on the power. Much to my relief, it seemed to have done the trick. The hardest part now was waiting for the next chat hour to re-establish contact and let the others know that all was okay aboard Joseph Young.

The next five days passed relatively quickly, and by December 15 I was 4,900 miles out of Cape Town, with only 1,600 miles to go before arriving in Sydney. If everything went well, I expected to be ashore in less than two weeks.

The night before I had received the absolutely best, most exciting news that I could have possibly imagined. I had placed a call through Perth Radio to Vicki at seven in the evening. Back in Canada it was seven o'clock on Sunday morning. Vicki promptly, if sleepily, answered the phone, and after a few minutes she broke her news: the day before she had booked a flight to Sydney, and would be arriving there on January 4. It was as if I had been given a new lease on life. After nearly four months apart, we would be together again in less than three weeks. Nothing was going to stand in my way now! Up on the foredeck later that day, half under water, cold and wet, I changed sails with renewed purpose. Instead of the usual stream of curses directed at everything and everyone, I found I was singing at the top of my lungs. Every mile I sailed now was bringing me closer to, rather than farther from, the one I loved.

On the morning chat hour I blurted out my good news to the others, unable to contain myself. It seemed that everybody's wives and families were meeting them in Australia, and I could join in their excited anticipation, rather than listening enviously as they made plans for the holidays.

From the latest Argos positions that day at noon, I saw that Hal Roth on *American Flag* was going to pass very close to me as I angled north towards him. Both of us were making for King Island at the western entrance to the Bass Straits. Accordingly, I agreed to leave my VHF radio on throughout the night, on the off chance that we might actually sight each other. The wind had gone very light, and except for a three-hour sleep before midnight, I was forced to stay at the helm trying to keep *Joseph Young* moving. When I heard Hal calling me at about two in the morning I dashed below to answer the radio. He reported that he had a light in sight to the east-south-east, and wondered if it was me. Racing back on deck, I peered into the night; sure enough, the lights of a small boat were visible off my port quarter. To make positive identification I asked Hal to flash his lights on and off a few times while I watched from the cockpit. It was definitely him! It was really exciting to have another competitor so close, and we talked frequently throughout the day. Hal's larger yacht gradually overhauled me as the day wore on, and by early evening his sail was lost to view.

The first of the Class-One boats had arrived in Sydney over

forty-eight hours earlier, and every day the size of the fleet at sea was steadily shrinking. The last five hundred miles of this leg filled me with trepidation, and I decided that one advantage of being at the back of the pack was that I could glean information from the boats up ahead. The problems would begin, I reckoned, as I approached King Island. This landfall marked the end of the open ocean. From here to Sydney I would be sailing in coastal waters, through the straits between Tasmania and Australia and then up the shore to the finish line. Single-handed sailing in confined waters such as these was a different ball game altogether. With land always in sight or just over the horizon, naps would have to be kept very short in case the self-steering allowed the boat to wander off course. Add to this the hazard posed by merchant ships and fishing boats, not to mention the many oilrigs drilling in the waters just off the eastern exit from the Bass Straits, and it would take a steady nerve indeed to be able to go below and fall asleep. With the satellite navigator still working spasmodically, the whole thing could shape up into a real nightmare! As far as I could see, the only opportunity for a sleep of any kind lay just after I passed King Island, where a stretch of about fifty miles was relatively free of navigational hazards. From here, with a favourable wind, it should be less than three days to Sydney. Although King Island itself was still almost 1,000 miles to the east, I began planning my passage accordingly.

On December 18 *Joseph Young* was thundering along in the worst sea conditions of the entire trip to date. The swells rolling in from the west were absolutely enormous, towering at least sixty feet above the deck as they rushed up from astern. With a wry grin, I imagined that the southern oceans were having one last crack at me before I reached shelter. In the early hours of the afternoon I saw a spectacular sight that I hoped was a good omen for the remaining portion of my trip to Sydney. About three hundred feet astern of the boat, with no warning, three sea mammals—large porpoises or small whales—exploded out of the water in unison. Leaping almost thirty feet clear of the sea, perfectly in synchronization with one another, they each followed a graceful arc, landing head first with hardly a splash. Awestruck, I gazed aft, but saw no further sign of their presence.

The weather continued to deteriorate, and by evening I knew it was merely a matter of time before the mainsail would have to come down entirely. The time for the chat hour was rapidly approaching, however, and I thought I could hold on until I had spoken with the other boats. What I heard on the radio that evening was the first indication of impending tragedy among us.

Jean-Luc Van Den Heede, sailing the French yacht *Let's Go*, came on the air and expressed his concern for Jacques de Roux aboard *Skoiern IV*. He explained that he, Jacques, and another French competitor, Guy Bernadin, had maintained a private radio schedule, talking three times a day in addition to the regular chat hour. Jacques had not been heard from in almost twenty-four hours. If it had been any of the other sailors, it might not have been as worrying, but if any one of us could have been considered a professional, it was Jacques. A career in the French Navy had made him a disciplined navigator. He knew the value of a regular radio schedule, and the implications of missing it. His prolonged silence surely indicated trouble. There were, however, as I knew personally, any number of reasons why one might fail to make a scheduled radio contact. A broken radio, an electrical problem on board, or simply sleeping through an alarm were all possibilities. Too, injury or illness might have kept him off the air. All these things had to be considered, and were discussed by the rest of us that evening. We agreed to wait until morning and see what the next Argos report showed as Jacques's most recent position. Guy Bernadin was due to arrive in Sydney within a matter of hours, and he would relay all our concerns to Race Headquarters. At this point, there was nothing further we could do.

After shutting down the radio, I had to hurry back on deck to deal with the sails. The wind was gusting well over 50 knots and had shifted to the west-south-west, meaning I would have to gybe the boat. The seas were absolutely horrendous, and I first set about getting the mainsail lowered completely. Balancing on the heaving deck with both hands free to secure the sail to the boom was tricky. I had just about finished the job when the crest of a breaking wave crashed aboard, catching me unaware. I didn't have a chance. As the water reached knee depth, my feet were swept from under me and down I went. Arms out to break the fall, I closed my eyes as my face went underwater. Washed across the deck, I felt the lifelines come up hard against my chest and instinctively grabbed on. Feeling my mouth clear of the water now, I opened my eyes again and took a breath. Both legs were under the lifelines, hanging overboard. Bruised, but otherwise allright, I hauled myself out from under the rail and crawled back aft to the cockpit. I had come awfully close to putting my safety harness to the real test. With only the small headsail up now, gybing the boat was a much safer manoeuvre, and within ten minutes I was back down below, stripping off sodden clothes. Definitely an occasion for a hot toddy!

Crawling into the quarterberth a short time later, I found that sleep did not come easily. I said a silent prayer for Jacques.

I was up early the following morning: with the storm still raging outside and my mind churning with thoughts of Jacques, I wasn't abe to sleep. I couldn't eat either — breakfast consisted of a pot of coffee, following which I dressed for the weather and made my way on deck. Heavy rain showers sweeping across the deck jarred me to my senses quicker than any cold shower could. The wind was gusting a good 60 knots and the seas had increased accordingly. All in all, it looked like it was going to be a pretty miserable day.

By noon there was still no concrete news of *Skoiern IV*, though the morning Argos report showed that Jacques's boat was heading south-south-east at a mere 4 knots. The Sydney finish line lay some 240 miles to the north of his position; it looked like *Skoiern IV* was drifting.

It was with a feeling of real dread that I tuned in to the chat hour that evening. All of our worst fears had been realized; *Skoiern IV* had been boarded that afternoon by the crew of a merchant ship helping in the search. Jacques was not on board. I turned off the radio. I found I was weeping, and I didn't want to talk to anyone.

Although I had not known Jacques well, the sense of loss was great. I had been tied up alongside *Skoiern IV* in Newport for two weeks prior to the start of the race, and we had shared a few laughs and the odd cup of coffee as we worked on preparations for the first leg. He had given Vicki and me the grand tour of his boat. It was the feeling of camaraderie that had grown between all the competitors in the race that made his loss so hard to accept. It was a very private sadness shared by those of us sailing in the BOC race.

By the following afternoon the gale had eased somewhat, and I raised the mainsail once more. We were making good progress, which was encouraging, but I was not keen on the timing for my landfall at King Island. I still had about two hundred miles to go, so things could change, but the way it was shaping up I would be passing the island shortly before midnight on December 21. If the visibility was impaired by rain I would have to hope for a timely fix from the satellite navigator. Approaching land was always nerve-wracking and tonight it was crucial that I get a good sleep.

I turned in early, fortified by a strong hot toddy, my last of the trip. Although the alarm clock woke me periodically, the conditions stayed fairly steady and I was able to return quickly to the warmth of the bunk.

At ten in the morning I saw my first ship since leaving Cape Town. A large tanker, she was headed west, presumably having passed through the Bass Straits. In the heavy swell she was rolling slowly and heavily. Content just to watch, I made no attempt to contact her on the radio.

As the afternoon waned my excitement at the possibility of sighting land that night increased. Sleep was out of the question, and I spent several hours scanning the charts that covered the final five hundred miles, noting the particular dangers and navigational marks. A satellite fix early in the evening gave my confidence a boost, and I adjusted course accordingly, hoping to pass close enough to sight the flash of the lighthouse as I passed north of King Island. The night sky was clouded over, but the visibility was quite good. Once past this first danger I could breathe a sigh of relief and, I hoped, grab a quick nap.

By 2300 hours there was still nothing. Standing aft in the cockpit I nervously scanned the horizon ahead, willing the light to show itself where I calculated it should be. The wind was back up to gale force, and the shallower water of the continental shelf was making the seas that much steeper. Suddenly, there it was, off the starboard bow. Not the light itself, but the loom of the beam as it swept across the sky. Carefully timing the sequence confirmed that it was King Island. Australia at long last.

About an hour passed from the time I first sighted the light until it lay safely astern. *Joseph Young* was now officially in the Bass Straits. Setting a course for due east on the auto-pilot, I trimmed the sails for the new heading and thankfully climbed back down below for a last look at the chart. I had clear sailing for a few hours on this course, and with full navigation lights and the VHF radio turned on, I began to strip off my oilskins in preparation for a short sleep. It was not to be. A sudden loud crash echoed through the boat, followed by the sound of violently flogging canvas. Hauling my clothes back on, I dashed, cursing, for the companionway steps. On deck, the end of the boom was lying across the leeward rail, trailing disconsolately in the water. The third reefing pennant had broken. Winching the boom up with the topping lift, I hustled to get the sail down before it too was damaged. As I surveyed the situation, I vented my frustration at whatever twist of fate it was that always seemed to bring about such problems just as one contemplated sleep.

The rough weather turned a simple repair job into a time-consuming struggle, and by the time I had the mainsail back up and drawing, daylight was almost upon us. My one chance for a solid sleep before arriving in Sydney had evaporated. I prayed that the wind would stay fair for the next few days, and thanked my lucky stars that I still had a good store of coffee on board. It was now twenty-four hours since last I had slept.

Sailing under an almost blue sky for the first time in days, I passed Rodondo Island at 1610 in the afternoon. This magnificent piece of rock, rising almost vertically several hundred feet from the water and covering only a few square miles, marked the eastern limits of the Bass Straits. From here, another thirty miles would take me clear of the island group scattered off to the east. It was a strange feeling indeed to be gazing at the Australian continent only a mile or two distant from the deck of *Joseph Young*. Our home waters seemed so very far away and I was stirred by pride at how well my small sloop had done to get us this far.

A very rough sea was still running, though it was different in character from those of only a few days before. The fronts of the waves were rising in perfectly straight lines, funnelled perhaps by the land. The crests were breaking in unison over widths of hundreds of yards, like surf on the beach, the hissing of the water carrying clearly across the wind. It was a dangerous sea, unlike any I had seen before.

Shortly after dark I rounded Hogan Island and came on to a north-easterly course that would lead me to Gabo Island, right on the south-east corner of the mainland, some 150 miles distant. Before I arrived there I would have to cross a major shipping lane and thread my way through the oilfield. The risk of collision ruled out the possibility of any sleep.

Approaching the shipping lane just before midnight, I felt like a cat trying to get across a highway. The lights of at least three ships were visible at all times, and I had to make several large alterations in course to keep out of their way. If nothing else, the resulting flow of adrenalin kept fatigue at bay.

On the evening of December 23, at 1920 hours, *Joseph Young* and I sailed quietly past Gabo Island Lighthouse in a gentle south-westerly breeze to begin the last 260-mile stretch up the coast to Sydney. The gale-force, or near gale-force winds that had been with us for so many days now had finally abated. Through the binoculars, I stared at the rocky promontory upon which the light had been built. It was here, in the first BOC Challenge in 1982, that the race had ended for one of the competitors. Exhausted, he had overslept and been driven on to the rocks by the current and a shifting wind. A chill crept over me at the thought. I vowed not to crawl into my bunk before *Joseph Young* was safely tied to the dock. The fact that I hadn't closed my eyes for nearly three days made me that much more afraid. In my present state I knew that once I fell asleep, no alarm clock on earth would be able to rouse me. With luck I would reach Sydney in another thirty-six hours. I simply had to hang on and hope for a fair wind.

Sitting up on the cockpit coaming, leaning back against the lifelines, I watched the lights of towns and villages, less than a mile off on the port side, slip by in the darkness. It was becoming a struggle to stay awake, and I found my mind wandering. With a jerk I sat bolt upright, the hair on the nape of my neck rising — I had heard the unmistakable sound of someone exhaling loudly right behind me! Spinning around, eyes wide, I peered over the rail. Under the water I saw a movement, and jumped back with a start as a large dolphin broke the surface and blew. Feeling a little foolish, I watched as half a dozen of the creatures gradually appeared and swam alongside for a while. As always, I was captivated by their beauty and was sorry when they finally vanished from sight.

When the sun came up in the morning it brought with it a change of climate that was almost unbelievable. On the chat hour, the competitors who had gone before had all remarked how it seemed, when they had rounded Gabo Island, that they had passed into a completely different world. Gone were the grey skies, the monstrous swells, the persistent cold, and the wicked gales. It was like being transported from the Arctic Ocean to the tropics in the blink of an eye. The water now was a beautiful blue, the sun beat down from a clear sky, and the temperature soared. Peeling off foul-weather gear and layers of thermal underwear, I dug out shorts, sneakers, and a T-shirt. The rigging was soon festooned with sodden bedding and woollen clothing of every description. Sailing close inshore to avoid the south-setting current farther out, I marvelled at the fantastic beaches and the thick vegetation. It was hard to believe that this was Christmas Eve, a time, in my experience, for snow and cold!

As the afternoon came on, the second wind that I had felt at dawn faded, and exhaustion began to overtake me. Despite the fact that the open ocean stretched out for hundreds of miles on my starboard side, I couldn't shake the feeling that I was sailing up a channel. I kept returning to the table to pore over the chart, finding it more and more difficult to orientate myself with respect to the land. My eyes felt as if they were full of sand, and the glaring sun and heat, which had been so welcome in the morning, were now taking their toll. I knew that what I desperately needed was sleep, but the more tired I became, the greater was my fear of not waking until it was too late. I was convinced that disaster was lurking just around the corner, waiting for me to lie down. It was a bizarre sensation.

Christmas Eve, almost midnight. My last night at sea for a while, I hoped. Tuned to a local FM radio station, I listened to

Christmas carols. Even they could do little to raise my spirits. The wind had dropped since dusk, and although I was only sixty miles from the finish line, at this speed it would be twenty hours before I could drop the sails for the last time. It looked like my goal of finishing this leg in under forty days was slipping out of reach.

At one o'clock in the morning, December 25, I wrote in the log-book the first entry for the day. It read, *Becalmed. Great. Merry Christmas.* Thoroughly dejected, I crawled back on deck to keep a lookout and wait for even the slightest breeze. The thought of having to endure another day of this was almost too much to bear. What happened next remains a bit of a mystery to me.

I came to with a start. I was perched on the starboard lifelines —stark naked! I had fallen asleep, my head on my knees, having removed my safety harness and clothes somewhere along the way. Badly shaken, I hurried below to put on a pot of coffee and bring myself to my senses. I looked at the time and saw that several hours had passed without my knowing. Cautiously I crept back on deck for a look around. Off to the east the sun was still below the horizon but the night was rapidly giving way to dawn. To the west, land was barely visible a few miles away. I had given myself a hell of a fright with this turn of events, and gathering up harness and clothes from the cockpit I realized how lucky I had been. Tripping on something, I stared in amazement; my flashlight was jammed down in the drain. It took a good tug to pull it free. What on earth had I been doing? Retreating below, I poured a cup of coffee and put my clothes back on. This sort of behaviour just wouldn't do!

By 0800 hours we were moving slowly northward again under the influence of a light southerly wind. I had the large #1 Genoa poled out to port, nicely balancing the mainsail. We were back in close to the shore, and with only forty miles to go I prayed that the wind would pick up a little and stay out of the south. Promptly at 0900 hours, I picked up the VHF radio and placed a call to Race Headquarters in Sydney. It was a real relief to hear a friendly voice, and to receive a few words of encour-

A final toast aboard *Joseph Young* before heading out, with my
mother Mary Hughes. Photo credit: John Mellamby

Joseph Young on August 30, 1986, minutes before starting gun sounded. Photo credit: John Mellamby

Three weeks out of Newport, still on first leg, making morning coffee.

Again on first leg, enjoying light winds in the North Atlantic (*above*) and changing the head sail (*below*).

On the doldrums, as one of many squalls approaches.

Joseph Young is greeted by porpoises in the South Atlantic shortly before reaching Capetown.

An albatross at sunset is observed during departure from Capetown.

Sailing towards Sydney—and playful dolphins—on Christmas Eve 1986.

Hal Roth (*American Flag*), Margaret Roth and Harry Mitchell aboard his *Double Cross* just after Harry arrived in Sydney. Photo credit: Vicki McDermott

Vicki and John having dinner with their Australian hosts. (From left: John, Vicki, Tracey, Bév, Wayne and Brian Hunter). Photo credit: Brian Hunter

Sydney's Birkenhead Point, January 1987, the scene one hour before start of third leg. Australia's Prime Minister Robert Hawke is aboard the French boat (Class I) *Ecureuil d'Aquitaine*. Photo credit: Vicki McDermott

Mark Schrader of Seattle, Washington aboard *Lone Star*, in Sydney, January 1987. Photo credit: Vicki McDermott

At an award ceremony in Sydney, January 1987—from left, Pentti Salmi (Finland), Mike Plant (USA), Hal Roth (USA), Mark Schrader (USA) in rear, Harry Mitchell (UK), Harry Harkimo (Finland), John Hughes (Canada), Richard Konkolski (USA), Ian Kiernan (Australia), Jean Yves Terlain (France), Philippe Jeantot (France) and Bertie Reed (South Africa). Photo credit: Vicki McDermott

Two days after the dismasting—showing the hole in the deck.

The jury rig—showing how the spinnaker poles were stepped on deck.

Sail repairs on the final leg.

Trying to dry out in the cold of the Southern Ocean, three weeks after dismasting.

At the end of the race, Hughes hands in his log book to Robin Knox-Johnston. Photo credit: Vicki McDermott

Heading south for wind shortly after the decision to head for Cape Horn.

Heading for Cape Horn after the dismasting.

In the Falkland Islands Military Warehouse, the new mast is ready to be stepped by (from left) Evert Bastet, Hughes and John Sandford.

Thanks to teasing puffs of wind, it takes eight hours to cover the last 10 miles to the finish line, in May 1987. Photo credit Vicki McDermott

Arriving off East Cove, Falkland Islands, March 1987. Photo credit:
British Forces Press

Rear Admiral Chris Leyland welcomes Hughes to the Falkland
Islands. Photo credit: British Forces Press

In January 1988, Hughes was awarded the Perkins Engines Trophy
which is given for feats of outstanding seamanship. Here, HRH
Princess Royal presents the trophy to John Hughes. (Photo credit:
Perkins Engines)

Joseph Young drifting towards the finish line, Newport harbour, May 1987. Photo credit: Vicki McDermott

agement. When pressed for an estimated time of arrival, however, the best I could do was tell them where I was and what the wind was like at present. While I was talking, a sudden loud flap from the sails sent a shudder through the boat. Quickly terminating the call, I hurried on deck to see what was going on. To my surprise, *Joseph Young* was now sailing backwards. The wind had shifted instantly through 180 degrees and was now blowing from dead ahead. With the boom held out by a preventer, and the spinnaker pole rigged for the headsail, we were going astern at about 3 knots! This was potentially dangerous. It seemed to take ages to get the boat sorted out and heading off on the port tack with the sails trimmed properly. Iwas well aware that I was reacting like a punch-drunk boxer. I was beyond tiredness, and stayed on my hands and knees as I moved about the deck. The breeze had increased slightly with the change in direction, which was the good news, the bad news being that I would now have to tack back and forth all the way to Sydney.

Two hours later I was crouched on the bow of the boat, sobbing with frustration and fatigue as I struggled to change the #1 for the #3 jib. The wind was increasing rapidly and I felt that life was just bloody unfair. This was turning into a repeat of my arrival in Cape Town, where I had had to beat straight into a gale to reach port.

By evening *Joseph Young* was punching into a rough sea, and I knew that I would be crossing the finish line in darkness. Ahead, I could see the cliffs that marked the entrance to Sydney harbour, but it was very nearly 2300 hours before I had worked my way that far north. By then, of course, I was in contact with Robin Knox-Johnston on board the Committee boat at the finish. I was also very confused, due largely to being utterly exhausted. To enter the harbour and reach the finish line, I first had to pass through a wide break in the cliffs known as Sydney Heads. The chart showed a flashing light on either side of this gap. From the deck of *Joseph Young*, a mile offshore, I could pick out only the light marking the southern Head. Knowing that my judgement was impaired by fatigue, and dazzled by the lights of the city in the background, I was terrified of making a mistake. Over the radio, I told Robin of my fears and said that I refused to head in for the land without being absolutely certain that I was where I thought I was. Visions of *Joseph Young* being smashed to pieces on the rocks ran through my mind. I suggested that perhaps I would head offshore, and return in daylight. For what happened next I will be forever in Robin's debt. Telling me to hang on, he brought the Committee boat out between the cliffs. Once in position, he pointed his searchlight to the east and flashed an agreed-upon signal. From out to sea, I gave a shout of relief as I saw the wink of his light, beckoning me in to safety. Grabbing the radio mike, I let him know I was on my way.

Ten minutes later, I was racing in past the harbour entrance, flanked by the Committee boat and a police launch. Blinded by their lights, disorientated by the noise and activity, the first indication I had of having crossed the finish line was the wail of their sirens. Thankfully, I luffed into the wind and rushed forward to douse the jib. Unfortunately, however, the self-steering had developed a small fault less than an hour before and now, with the helm unattended, we began to bear off, which allowed the wind to catch the mainsail. Hurriedly stowing the jib, I dashed back aft, shouting a warning to the police launch which now lay directly in front of a rapidly accelerating *Joseph Young*. Except for their quick action, I would have had the distinction of being the first BOC yacht to ram the welcoming police boat!

Disaster momentarily averted, I dropped the mainsail and gratefully caught the tow line tossed over from the launch. The second leg of the race was over. The time was ten minutes to midnight, Christmas Day; thirty-nine days, twenty-three hours, and fifty minutes since the starting gun had been fired in Cape Town. By the skin of my teeth I had made it within my target of forty days.

It took almost an hour for the tow to arrive at Birkenhead Point Marina, where we were all to be berthed during our stay in Australia. As we sailed past the lights of the Sydney Opera House and under the famous Harbour Bridge, it gradually sank in that for the next few weeks I could relax. Mark Shrader and his wife, Michelle, and Hal Roth and his wife, Margaret, were waiting at my berth to take the lines. I was deeply touched that they had come out in the middle of the night to greet me. After handshakes and hugs all round they dragged me aboard *Lone Star* for a celebratory drink while I filled out the requisite customs forms. I was tired—overwhelmingly tired—but the feeling of being ashore and among friends once again was simply unbeatable. Laughing and joking about our recent hardships, I realized a tremendous sense of satisfaction at having safely completed a crossing of the southern oceans.

As soon as the Committee boat had docked, Robin Knox-Johnston joined us aboard Mark's yacht. With him were two young Australians, a brother and sister, who were introduced to me as Wayne and Tracy Hunter. Robin explained that Wayne, a member of the Short-Handed Sailing Association of Australia, an association of solo and pairs sailors, had volunteered to be my host while I was in Sydney, and that I would be spending the night with his family. I am sure that, looking at me, Wayne wondered what he had got himself into. I was still in my foul-weather gear, wet, sunburned, with (so I was told later) a crazed look in my red-rimmed eyes, sunken-faced, and probably smelling like a bag of dirty laundry. By now it was almost one o'clock in the morning, I was nearly incoherent with fatigue, and Wayne wanted to get me home. Grabbing a few things, I said good-night to the crowd and staggered off to his car.

The next thing I remember is waking up in the back seat with Wayne and his father, Brian, trying to make me get get out of the car and stand up. I followed them into the house to meet Bev, Wayne and Tracy's mother. Bev had kept a Christmas dinner hot for me, and asked what I would like first; a meal, a shower, or some sleep. The look of relief on all their faces when I said a shower was obvious! Hustling me off to the bathroom, they told me to take as long as I wanted and I was soon revelling in the luxury of unlimited hot water.

Forty minutes later, the family stood worriedly gathered outside the bathroom door. The shower was running, but there were no sounds of movement from me. I was, in fact, slumped in the shower stall, fast asleep. I woke up, calling "Just coming," as the door opened. The Hunters must have thought Canadians were a strange breed, but they sat me down to eat and plied me with questions as I wolfed down the best Christmas meal ever. As soon as I was finished, they led me to a spare bedroom, where without further ado I crawled between the sheets and passed out.

The first half of the single-handed around-the-world BOC Challenge was truly behind me. From here on in, every mile sailed would take me closer to home. My confidence in myself and in *Joseph Young* had grown in leaps and bounds over the last four months. Nothing would stop me now.

PART THREE

Sydney to the Falkland Islands

My first night ashore in Australia was sweet but too short. Though I'd gone without sleep for days, I was up just after seven the next morning; Bertie Reed the South African competition was due to arrive in port that day, and I was determined to be there when he crossed the finish line. I also wanted to check on *Joseph Young* and to start organizing the jobs that needed to be done before the start of the next leg. Vicki was flying in from Canada in nine days, and I planned to have as much of the work completed as possible before then.

Over breakfast, I apologized to the Hunter family for my appearance the night before, as well as for turning up late for Christmas dinner. Bev Hunter laughed off my embarrassment, and exclaimed that I seemed to her to be much taller today. She had assumed that I stood only about five feet the night before, when I had arrived at her house slouched over with fatigue.

After eating, Wayne and I set off in his van for the marina. Clad in shorts and a shirt, I marvelled at the warm weather and drank in my first glimpse of Sydney. For years, Australia had been number one on my list of countries I wanted to visit, and to have arrived the hard way made being here doubly satisfying. After a short drive we pulled up to Birkenhead Point, where the boats were moored, and headed off to the BOC office. Checking in, I picked up my mail and the official information package pertaining to our stopover. We then strolled down to the docks to open up *Joseph Young* and haul off the accumulated laundry. It took a while to reach my boat; there were emotional reunions as I bumped into some of the other skippers. Since we had left Newport, our numbers had been whittled down from twenty-five to eighteen, and those of us still in the running had been drawn closer as a result.

After cleaning out the worst of the mess aboard *Joseph Young*, Wayne and I headed off to join the growing crowd up in the office. Boxing Day was the start of the famous Sydney-to-Hobart yacht race, and John Biddlecombe, the Australian who had had to drop out of the BOC race on the first leg, was taking us out on his diving tug to watch the start. Bertie Reed was due in shortly after that, and we planned to welcome him in.

Steaming out to Sydney Heads gave me my first look at the harbour in daylight. It is a huge harbour and we were one of literally hundreds of spectator boats massed at its entrance to watch the race start. When the gun sounded and the maxi-yachts charged across the line on their way to Tasmania, all hell broke loose! The spectator fleet raced after them honking and cheering, and how collisions were avoided was beyond me. It was quite a spectacle.

After the excitement was all over, we retired to a small cove in the harbour for lunch and to wait for news of Bertie's approach. When it came, we headed out to meet *Stabilo Boss*— and our tug caught fire! Though we quickly put out the fire with the fire extinguishers on board, we were left disabled and drifting, able, from a quarter of a mile away, to watch Bertie cross the finish line, unaware of our presence. By the time a police launch had towed us back to the marina, he was already tied up and finished with customs. So much for our big welcome.

That night I returned to the Hunters' house excited at the prospect of making a phone call home. Unfortunately, the excitement barely won out over the exhaustion. The time difference made it necessary to wait until almost midnight in Australia for the sun to rise in Canada. Having had only a five-hour nap since arriving ashore, I was groggy with fatigue by the time Vicki and I finally talked and, I don't think I made a lot of sense.

Afterwards, however, I tottered off for a full twelve hours' sleep, more than content.

For the remainder of the week, Wayne and I worked long and hard to ready *Joseph Young* for the next leg of the race. Rigging was replaced, winches cleaned and greased, the satellite navigator taken off for repair, and every item of gear checked for wear. Relatively speaking, I had come through virtually unscathed, but there were still lots of jobs to be completed. I had decided to have the boat hauled out of the water here in Australia. We were now halfway around the world, and an inspection and painting of the underwater hull were past due. Negotiating with the owner of the boatyard just around the corner, we arrived at a fair price for the work. He first asked if I was sponsored; I wasn't. He then deliberated for some time, before quoting me the cost with a wide grin; one case of Foster's, well chilled—another example of Aussie generosity, something that I found was far from rare.

The days passed quickly, and New Year's Eve was upon us. The Race Committee had chartered a tour boat for the evening, and the party began as soon as we left the dock. Most of the competitors and their wives were there, and we danced and drank our way down the harbour. The grand finale was a fireworks display from the cliffs overlooking the water, followed by a rousing rendition of "Auld Lang Syne." Wayne and I decided against driving that night (out of concern for whoever else might be out on the road) and walked over to *Joseph Young* to spend the remaining few hours of darkness asleep there.

Four days later, Vicki finally arrived Down Under. Wayne had agreed to drive me to the airport, and, at my insistence we were standing in the terminal a full hour before her flight was due. *Nervous* was an understatement for the way I felt. It had been over four months since Vicki and I had last seen each other, and my stomach was in knots. Passengers at last started to emerge from the customs area, but no Vicki. Had she missed the plane? Would she really be here? At last I saw her — at another exit several hundred feet away. I took off like a flash. She barely saw me coming before I swung her in my arms. I wanted Vicki and me to have some time alone together and consequently I had arranged a short vacation for us away from the activity of the marina and the city. For the next few days we strolled on beaches, swimming, laughing, and catching up. But too soon it was time to return to the business of preparing for sea. Once again, the Hunters came through with flying colours. Vicki and I were to stay with them for the duration of our time together in Australia, and we were made to feel as part of the family. Wayne gave all of his time to helping on *Joseph Young* for the ten days left before the start of the third leg. With Vicki working hard alongside us, the job list was quickly whittled down.

On January 10, *Double Cross*, carrying Harry Mitchell, the English competitor, crossed the finish line to signal the official end of the second leg of the BOC Challenge. All competitors were now in port. After his difficulties and injuries, it was with heartfelt relief that we welcomed Harry in. Like me, Harry arrived in the middle of the night, exhausted after a long struggle up the coast. His wife, Diana, had flown in several days before. Vicki and I, along with a small band of others, kept a vigil with her during the evening waiting word of his approach. Aboard *Joseph Young*, while Vicki made tea, I tried to raise Harry on the radio. When at last I succeeded, I handed the microphone over to his wife. Talking to Diana he sounded all but done in, anxious to reach safety and have this portion of the voyage behind him.

When he was finally within striking distance of the finish, we all boarded a motor launch to go out and meet him, and an hour later, *Double Cross* was under tow up the harbour, Harry shying from the glare of camera lights. At the dock, a sizeable crowd was on hand to greet him, but when they, the reporters, and the customs officials finally dispersed, Diana and Harry, Michelle and Mark Shrader, Hal and Margaret Roth, and Vicki and I sat in the cockpit and shared a quiet drink as the early light of dawn crept across the sky. It was good to be among friends, all sharing a common bond.

During the last week of our stay in Sydney, Vicki and I avoided the subject of our approaching separation. Instead, we worked long hours on the boat and made time for a little sight-seeing. One beautiful morning we boarded a train for the Blue Mountains, so named for the steamy haze that shrouded them, to spend the day with an Australian friend we had met in Canada. We hiked through the bush, swimming in the river when the heat became unbearable. Not wanting to leave Australia without seeing a kangaroo or a koala, we took another day off to visit a wildlife park. Later in the week, for a kind of busman's holiday, we took *Joseph Young* out for a sail, using the opportunity to fine-tune the rig for the upcoming voyage.

The start was set for the afternoon of January 18. On the morning of the seventeenth, I filed in to the obligatory skippers' briefing along with the other sixteen competitors. (*Thursday's Child*, sailed by Warren Luhrs from the United States, had withdrawn after breaking his mast in the harbour only two days before.) The mood was one of cautious optimism, despite the recent tragic loss of Jacques de Roux, to whom we had said our last good-byes earlier at a memorial service held in the nearby Naval Chapel. Now we were looking ahead to Cape Horn. Speaking for myself, I felt that having come safely halfway around the world was reason enough for a little confidence. I was certain that if *Joseph Young* had had any faults they would have surfaced by now. The rest was up to me. With a cautious hand I had to guide her through the nine thousand miles of ocean between Sydney and Rio. I never, not for an instant, doubted that we would make it.

With the day's serious business out of the way, it was back to the boat to wrap up last-minute preparations. Vicki and Wayne had been hard at it throughout the morning, and by the time I arrived the mounds of food and other stores had miraculously disappeared below into the various lockers and bins. All that remained was to top up the fresh water and diesel tanks, sort out some ropes on deck, and program the single-sideband (SSB) radio for the new frequencies. The atmosphere in the marina was crackling with tension as the hours ticked away — it became harder and harder to maintain an outward appearance of calm. As soon as possible, we escaped to the Hunters' for

101

some peace and quiet. There, the rest of the afternoon slipped quickly by with postcard-writing, packing, and getting ready for our last night ashore.

The Race Committee had laid on the prize-giving ceremonies and dinner that evening in a theatre-restaurant on the harbour shore. It was a great way to wrap up our three weeks on land and get us in a good frame of mind for tomorrow. With music, dinner, dancing, and fireworks, it was difficult to imagine that within twenty-four hours we would each be alone again on the high seas, our world reduced to the boat beneath us and the elements that drove it. We drank a toast to our reunion in Rio.

January 18 dawned fine and clear, a good omen I hoped. Towing out to the start area was due to begin at 1300 hours, preceded by a visit from Australia's prime minister. Vicki and the Hunters were booked on a ferry to watch the start, and Wayne was to accompany me aboard *Joseph Young* to help with the tow and raising sail. Inevitably, the moment I had been dreading most arrived all too quickly. Vicki and I must say good-bye and face up to the prospect of another four-month separation. In many ways it was easier this time than it had been in Newport. Both of us had some idea now of what lay ahead. I knew that the sooner I got going, the sooner I would get home; and spurring me on was the knowledge that every mile under the keel now was one less mile between us. And, after the last two weeks, I knew in my heart that this was a beginning, not an end. None the less, such leave-takings are always emotional affairs. As Vicki walked away I watched until she was lost in the crowd. I then turned briskly back to *Joseph Young*, anxious to get under way; there was no longer anything for me here.

Out in the start area an hour and a half later, confusion reigned. Spectator boats had swamped the police patrols by their sheer numbers, and manoeuvring in the ensuing mêlée became a nightmare. Wayne and I had dropped the tow and raised the sails in good order, but there were less than ten minutes to go before the gun and the inflatable tenders that were supposed to take off crew were nowhere in sight. After an aborted attempt to transfer Wayne to a friendly motor cruiser, I sailed in towards the committee boat to seek help. Finally, after several calls on the radio and a lot of arm signals (not all of which followed proper nautical etiquette) a tender appeared, much to Wayne's relief. I don't know which worried him more, the idea of having to sail to Cape Horn with me, or being the reason for my disqualification. It was eight minutes after the official start, but I was on my way at last. Over towards the shore, I could see Vicki waving from the deck of the tour ship. I raised my arm in a final farewell, and watched until the tour ship faded to a mere speck on the horizon.

Leaving port, it never failed to amaze me how rapid was the transition from crowds and confusion to open sea and tranquillity. Within an hour, the land was no more than a thin dark line on the horizon astern, the steady north-east breeze carrying us steadily offshore. A mile or more to the south, I could see Mark and *Lone Star*, his blue and white spinnaker flying. Three other boats remained in view for a while too, but by sunset the sea belonged to *Joseph Young* alone. With darkness, the wind piped up quickly and I reduced sail accordingly. It was a short, sharp blow that lasted only until dawn, but it was the cause of a small problem for me and a big scare for Vicki.

I had turned in for some sleep just after midnight, only to wake up an hour later as the boat rounded up into the wind, sails flogging in protest. Leaping out of the bunk and up on deck, I was presented with the first failure of this leg. The wind-vane, which had been steering the boat, had thrown a bearing and two bolts and was trailing uselessly in its mount over the stern. Switching quickly over to the electronic auto-pilot, I settled back on course and went below to assemble the tools and spare parts I needed for the repair. The sea was quite rough by now, and in order to make the job a little safer, I brought *Joseph Young* around almost head-to-wind on a northerly course. Clambering right back aft on the stern, I stood in water up to my knees for about half an hour, working to install the new bearing. When it was completed, I once again resumed course with the windvane steering. Down in the galley, I put a kettle on to boil, and when the tea was brewed, sat back with a mug-up to while away a few minutes dreaming up all sorts of unpleasant things that could be done to the technicians ashore who had "overhauled" the windvane. Feeling a little better, I crawled back into the bunk for another attempt at sleep.

While I had struggled in the stern of a boat heading north, the opposite direction to my real course, miles above a satellite had passed overhead and read the transmission from my Argos beacon. Thus the information flashed back to Race Headquarters ashore was that *Joseph Young* was inexplicably off course.

At almost the same time, back in Sydney, Vicki was awakened by the howl of the wind as it rattled the windows of the Hunters' house. She could not help wondering if the same gale was blowing out at sea. When morning finally came, she called the race centre to see if there was any news. What they told her was all bad. Several of the boats had reported hard going in overnight winds of 50 knots. There had been no contact with me, and the Argos showed I was heading north. Tired, worried, still aching from yesterday's separation, she found it all too easy to reach the worst conclusion. With a flight to catch in a few hours, Vicki wouldn't know that I was allright until she phoned Australia from Los Angeles a nerve-wracking twelve hours later. As always, it was harder for the one left behind.

Meanwhile, out on the Tasman Sea, the winds had gone very light and remained that way for the next two days. Although I was frustrated by the slow speeds, *Joseph Young* did well in these conditions compared to the others, and was soon lying in third place in Class Two. The calm weather had some other advantages too. I was able to repair the electronic log (which had stopped working almost immediately after the start), and to reprogram the SSB radio to improve long-distance communications. The easy sailing also gave me lots of time to reflect on the stopover in Sydney, and to ponder the future. I found I was more depressed than I had at first thought I would be about being alone again. Preparing supper one night I found a card from Vicki hidden in the food locker. The next morning, a message written on the egg carton brought back a flood of memories. Absence was making the heart grow painful. However, I wasn't alone in my loneliness; talking to the other sailors on the chat hour, I found that all of us seemed to be suffering badly from the marina blues.

We didn't have long to mope, however. The third night out the weather provided a diversion in the form of a southerly gale that lasted for four days. Living conditions on board rapidly deteriorated as *Joseph Young* pounded into the seas. The going was extremely tough.

As the bow drove deep into the face of one particularly vicious wave, solid water rolled back across the deck bringing the boat to a virtual standstill. With the sound of a whip cracking the jib sheet parted, leaving the sail free to flog violently as it streamed out to leeward. Cursing, I crawled forward along the deck to douse the sail and rig a new sheet. By the time I had the job finished and was able to return to the relative protection of the cockpit I was soaked to the skin despite my oilskins. Hoisting the new sail, I scanned the boat for further damage and saw, to my utter disgust, that several of the slides that held the mainsail to the mast had also broken. Not fancying my chances of being able to sew replacement slides onto the sail under these conditions, I lashed the sail to the mast with some light line until such time as the weather moderated.

Poring over the latest weather maps, willing the barometer to rise—nothing seemed to work. The wind continued to blow, the waves continued to crash against the hull with monotonous regularity. When the gale finally abated on January 26, my nerves were almost at breaking point, worn down by the continuous noise and the ever-present fear of disaster.

But, with the weather I soon had the bedding and wet clothes hung out to dry, the mainsail repaired, and was able to cook my first proper meal for several days. Rather than trying to conjure up a reason for retiring with grace, I was now looking forward to clearing New Zealand and running before the wind to Cape Horn. Like all sailors, I am blessed with a very short memory.

48 20S 165 52E

At six this morning I could see that this was going to be a perfect day's sailing. The sky was absolutely clear blue, and with the wind out of the west Joseph Young *was romping along at a comfortable speed, the sea behind us. Coffee in hand, music on the tape deck, and the smell of bacon in the frying pan: it couldn't get much better. To top it all off, I had a phone call to Canada scheduled for eleven o'clock. The Maritime Museum in Halifax had arranged a radio question-and-answer period from their auditorium, and I knew that Vicki and many of my friends would be there.*

When the call finally came through, I was beside myself with excitement, and, after establishing contact with the museum, managed to have a short private conversation with Vicki. Hearing her voice, knowing that she had made it home safely, was worth a month of fair winds.

That evening, as usual, I had the radio turned on a few minutes before eight in anticipation of the chat hour. At five after the hour I put out a call to *Lone Star* to see how Mark was faring. There was no reply. A little surprised, for Mark never missed the opportunity for a bull session, I spoke with Hal aboard *American Flag*. He, too, had been unable to raise Mark, but we were not unduly worried, for all had been well on *Lone Star* when Mark and I had talked that morning. For the next twenty minutes or so I listened as the other boats called one another. When the conversations finally petered out, I was reaching to shut down the radio when I heard Bertie Reed calling me from his position several hundred miles to the east. Like Mark, Bertie had a ham-radio licence. It seems that Mark had been absent from three pre-arranged schedules on that network since this morning. This shed a different light on the situation. *Lone Star* had now missed four contacts that day. Mark was becoming conspicuous by his silence. Bertie voiced the same concerns that were beginning to stir in me, and we discussed whether it might not be a good idea for a phone call to be placed to Race Head-quarters in Newport. Guy Bernadin suddenly broke in on the airwaves to urge us not to delay taking action. If it turned out that there was, in fact, no problem, no harm done, but if we did nothing and the unthinkable had happened, it would be an awful burden to carry. The decision made, I agreed to phone Newport. Bertie knew that Mark had another radio schedule with a New Zealand ham operator at one in the morning, and planned to listen in, hoping that Mark would show. I would meet Bertie on this frequency again at 0200 to compare notes. Having done all we could for now, we signed off the air.

Through Sydney Radio, I was able to reach Peter Dunning, one of the Race Committee members, at his home in Newport. The time there was five o'clock in the morning. After I had briefly explained the situation to him, Peter told me to call him at the office in an hour, by which time he would have the latest Argos information available on *Lone Star*. I shut off the radio.

The next hour passed with excruciating slowness. Based on a twelve-hour-old position, I altered course for a rough intercept with Mark. Although none of us mentioned it, the circumstances that had led up to the loss of Jacques de Roux just six weeks ago were fresh in our minds. Pacing the small cabin, I felt sick with worry. The not knowing was gnawing at my innards, along with a sense of inadequacy.

Eventually, at 2315 hours a second call was put through to Race Headquarters. The latest Argos report showed that Mark was approximately 120 miles to the south-south-east of my position, making a speed of 5.6 knots on a course of 123 degrees. That he was still moving at a reasonable speed in the right direction gave us a glimmer of hope. Perhaps he would show up on the radio at 0100 and put our fears to rest. In the meantime, I would continue to head in his direction, and maintain contact with Bertie and shore. It was back to the waiting game.

Two hours later the optimism I had felt after talking to shore was eroded by news from Bertie. Mark had failed to make an appearance on his radio schedule. This was turning into a real bloody nightmare. Without verbal contact with *Lone Star* it was not hard to imagine the self-steering in control of an empty boat. Returning to the cockpit of *Joseph Young*, I took over at the tiller, trying to coax a little more speed from her. It helped to keep busy. Around me, the sea looked dark and cold.

At 0530, I placed another call to Newport for an Argos update. *Lone Star* had apparently altered course 30 degrees towards the south, and increased speed by 1 knot. I really didn't know what to make of it. Our next chat hour was a little over an hour away; I would just have to hope and wait.

No sooner had I hung up the microphone than all hell broke loose on board *Joseph Young*. Slammed by a sudden squall, she lay right over on her side, throwing me into the settee. The violent flogging of the sails shook the boat like a bone in the teeth of a crazed dog. Fear catching in my throat, I slithered sideways up through the hatch and frantically cast off the sheets, allowing the wind to spill from the sails. Freed from the overpowering pressure, *Joseph Young* regained her equilibrium, and, suddenly as it had sprung up, the wind dropped, allowing me a chance to get everything under control again. Trembling, I gazed around in disbelief; everything was still intact. Moving slowly, I took a third, precautionary, reef in the mainsail. Another performance like that we didn't need!

At 0700, dread lying heavy on my heart, I switched on for the chat hour and put out a rather hollow call for *Lone Star*. Back came Mark's voice, chipper as ever! Relief turning instantly to anger, I cursed him for worrying us so. Mark explained that he had been laid out by a sudden, short, severe attack of the flu, and as the depth of our concern became apparent to him, he apologized in a broken voice. I felt as though I had just found a long-lost friend.

The next morning the chat hour brought yet another blow to morale. Harry Mitchell had gone aground on the south shore of New Zealand. Severely battered by high winds and heavy seas in the Tasman Sea, Harry had sensibly decided to put in for repairs. With a broken self-steering and generator problems, it would have been foolhardy to face five thousand miles of open ocean when help was so close at hand. A breakdown in communications, a nasty turn in the weather, and the failure of a crucial lighthouse had led to *Double Cross* running up on a beach only minutes from safety. Harry, fortunately, was not hurt, but he was forced to retire from the race.

With Harry gone, there were only sixteen of us left. Aboard *Joseph Young*, the events of the last two days had left me feeling a little drained. I had honestly believed, departing Sydney, that the worst was over. I tried to put myself in Harry's shoes; to have a long-standing dream shattered after enduring so much would be unbearably depressing. I thought that nothing, absolutely nothing, could be worse than having to overcome such an intensely personal defeat. That, in a nutshell, was why we were all out here alone in the first place. It was selfish, perhaps, but in our own way we were each probing the limits of our capabilities. We were trying to prove something, yes, but only to ourselves. To be denied the opportunity of finding the light at the end of one's personal tunnel would be devastating.

On the evening of February 5 I sat at the table, writing a letter home. I had spoken with Vicki on the phone the night before and was still savouring the contact. Outside, the weather was nearly perfect. After a period of mist this morning, the sky had cleared, and, with the wind from the west, we were running with the #2 jib poled out to port. The noon position had put me exactly halfway between Sydney and Cape Horn, cause enough for a little celebration. This afternoon I had sighted a small whale about 150 feet astern, the first sign of life in a while.

Having finished the letter, I was just about to crawl into the bunk for some sleep when a loud flap from the jib alerted me to a wind shift. It was uncanny how conditions could remain steady all day, then change just as one made a move towards the sleeping bag. Very reluctantly, I wormed into cold oilskins and ventured on deck. I peered at the compass, then at the sails, and decided that the breeze had gone to the west-north-west. Gybing the jib, I crawled up to the bow and took down the spinnaker pole, securing it firmly back to the deck. Altering course slightly, I then trimmed the sails for a broad reach, and watched with satisfaction as the speed crept up a notch. With a silent ''please'' to the wind to remain steady, I dodged back below. Easing into the quarterberth, I pulled the damp covers up around my neck, shivering slightly until some warmth was generated. Slowly, I drifted off into a less than perfect sleep.

Instantly awake, I lay still for a split second, my mind registering only noise, a terrible crash stretching into a drawn-out rumble. Jack-knifing out of the bunk, I slammed my head on the deck above. The pain went virtually unnoticed. Underneath me, I could feel a change in the way *Joseph Young* was moving, sluggishly, as if a great weight was bearing down upon her. I knew without a doubt that something had gone dreadfully wrong.

The pale greyness of early dawn filtered in through the portholes. Looking forward I hauled on my boots, and the enormity of the disaster that had befallen me became apparent. For the first time, I tasted real terror. "No. Oh, no," I whispered, over and over, as I slid back the hatch to confirm what I already knew —the mast had broken.

Sheared off flush with the deck, the butt of the mast had jumped off to port and driven down through the cabin top, punching a jagged hole into the interior of the boat. Falling quickly, the spar had then bent in an almost perfect right angle as it jammed in the hole. In the cabin, the bottom four feet of the mast was grinding around above the chart table. On deck, the remaining fifty-five feet was lying over the starboard side, held almost on the surface of the water by the port shrouds. All the rigging was still intact, as were the spreaders. Without her towering spread of sail above, *Joseph Young* looked naked, defenceless, the trailing wreckage giving her the appearance of a bird with a broken wing. (The wind hadn't been overly strong and there seemed no obvious reason for this horrendous event to have occurred. Later examination of the lower part of the mast came up with metal fatigue as the most likely cause.)

Shaking badly, my mind numbed with shock and fear, I scrambled feverishly to collect the bolt cutters and my knife. The normally neat cabin was a shambles; chunks of the shattered deck were scattered everywhere like broken glass, and water was splashing down through the hole as we wallowed in the swell. Regaining the deck, clad only in boots and underwear, I tried to think where to begin. A confusion of tangled ropes and rigging lay everywhere. All I knew for certain was that the biggest threat to my survival lay with the slowly sinking mast alongside. For the moment it was held quite firmly in place by the piece wedged through the deck and the straining shrouds. If it pulled clear and went completely overboard, it would become a deadly battering ram. With the multitude of lines holding it close to the boat, it could easily drive another hole in the hull, probably below the waterline. The consequences didn't bear thinking about. I knew that I had to cut the whole mess away before I found myself in real trouble, however, I was also

111

aware that whatever I could salvage would prove useful in the days ahead. With this in mind I attacked the boom first, working frantically to cut the foot of the mainsail clear. Next I grabbed a wrench from the tool box and set about trying to unbolt the boom from the mast. I had been at it for a mere ten minutes when *Joseph Young* rolled off a swell, throwing the base of the mast back out of the hole. Scrambling clear as it swung dangerously across the deck, I knew that my time was now very limited. Bolt cutters in hand, I dashed aft and began chopping away the rigging according to a hastily conceived plan. First to go was the backstay, followed quickly by the runners and checkstays. Given the strength of the damned, I found it surprisingly easy to cut through the heavy wire. Next, the boom vang and the maze of running rigging clustered around the base of the mast. The starboard shrouds were not carrying any weight, so they were cut too. To try and get forward past the bucking mast would have been fatal, so the forestay would have to wait till last. All that remained now were the port shrouds. Saying a silent prayer, I knelt down and sheared them all in rapid succession. Wide-eyed, I watched as the tangled mess bumped and scraped its way across the deck. With a final lurch it dropped overboard, carrying with it the port lifelines. Crouched frozen on deck, I listened for the crash of the mast punching a hole in the hull. Silence. After ten seconds, I realized that, for the time being anyway, I was safe. Total disaster had been averted. From up on the bow there was a sudden bang, like a gunshot, as the forestay parted. Unable to hold the weight of the entire rig as it hung underneath the boat, the turnbuckle had sheared in half. Except for a couple of blocks and the boom-vang tackle, everything above deck level aboard *Joseph Young* was now sinking towards the ocean floor, some two miles below. It had been less than thirty minutes since I had been so rudely awakened.

Looking around, I realized that *Joseph Young* was in a sorry state indeed. Forward, the starboard side of the bow pulpit was crushed down flat against the hull. The starboard lifelines had all gone, except for two bare stanchions. Amidships, water was still streaming below through the gaping hole in the deck. Along with the mast, I had also lost both radio antennas, and therefore all contact with the outside world. Fortunately the Argos beacon had survived, and I was much relieved to note that neither of the spinnaker poles, still lashed on deck, had been damaged. Things could have been worse.

Climbing gingerly down into the cabin, I sat down long enough to get a grip on myself and plan an immediate course of action. Priority number one was obviously to repair the hole in the deck, making *Joseph Young* watertight once again. If the weather was to breeze up, the pump would find it hard going to keep up with the influx of water. From stores brought along for just such an eventuality, I selected a four-foot-square piece of plywood and took it on deck. Without the weight of the mast and rigging aloft, the motion of *Joseph Young* had become unbelievably jerky as the lead keel flicked her upright after each wave. Standing up would have been impossible; even crawling on my hands and knees it was difficult to retain my balance. Lying the plywood over the hole, I marked out the lines for a proper patch, and returned below. With the handsaw, I cut the wood to shape and from a roll of soft rubber (also part of the emergency stores) I cut a gasket to the same pattern. Back on deck, I used the hand drill to make four holes through the patch and the deck, into which I shoved suitable bolts. From below I screwed on the washers and nuts, puzzled about how I could tighten them when I was able to work from only one side at a time. Vice-grips provided the answer. Clamping them onto the nut, and tying them off to the lower four feet of mast still occupying the cabin to prevent them turning, I used a wrench on deck to dog the bolts down firmly. With the patch in place, I sat down again, feeling quite pleased with myself.

Looking at the time, I realized that the chat hour was only three hours away. It was imperative that I make contact with the rest of the fleet at that time. After the recent episode with Mark, and the events leading up to the loss of Jacques, I could just picture the panic ashore if I didn't respond to the call. The noon Argos report, which would show that I had stopped moving, coupled with my radio silence would bring the Race Committee to the obvious conclusion that I was in serious trouble. Other competitors would be asked to proceed to my position and investigate. I certainly didn't want to be the cause of so much trouble.

I set about fashioning a makeshift antenna for the radio. From a spare main halyard, I cut off the fifty-foot section of wire I would need. This fitted nicely into the tuner's insulator, being almost the same diameter as the original backstay antenna. The big problem was how to hold it aloft. All I had to work with were the two spinnaker poles, the longest of which was only eighteen feet from end to end. Well, it would have to do. For the next hour I struggled to erect this new "mast" in the cockpit, managing to blacken a fingernail and give myself a nasty cut across the back of the hand in the process. The antenna I led from the stern, over the top of the pole, and down to the bow. Where it touched the pole, it was insulated with rubber and electrical tape.

With half an hour still to spare before the chat hour, I gratefully made my way below for a cup of hot, sweet coffee. Assuming that the radio would work, I now had to decide how I was going to answer the inevitable question from my fellow competitors. Did I want to be picked up? It would have to be now or never, for the chances of a ship passing through this area were very slim indeed. If I was going to get outside assistance, it would have to come from one of the other boats in the race, and I couldn't keep them waiting for a decision. Looking around the interior of *Joseph Young* was not encouraging. The bilges were full of water I would have to pump out, and water was still leaking in around the patch in the deck and around the port chainplate, which had opened up slightly under the strain of the dismasting. Chunks of fibreglass, bits of plywood, sawdust, and tools were strewn everywhere. On the bright side, I was no longer in immediate danger. The question really was: would I be able to construct some form of jury-rigged mast and sail unaided to land before running out of food or drinking water?

Thinking back over the last three years of hard work and long preparations, of dreams and expectations I had set for myself, I knew the question didn't even need to be asked. *Joseph Young* was not in any danger of sinking; I could not abandon her and give up on myself now. Failure was simply too bitter a pill to swallow.

At 0800 I turned on the radio, keeping my fingers crossed that my efforts with the antenna would give me sufficient range to reach at least one of the other boats. After a few minutes silence, Mark's voice filled the cabin, "*Joseph Young, Joseph Young*, this is *Lone Star, Lone Star*, do you read? Over." My heart pounding in my chest, I replied, "*Lone Star*, this is *Joseph Young*. Over." To my immense relief, Mark was able to hear me as clearly as ever. "Hey, John. How's everything going this morning?" he asked. Trying very hard to keep my voice under control, I responded, "Well, Mark, not too good. I lost the rig last night."

Over the course of the next ten minutes or so I passed along my position (52 47S 149 19W) for transmission to Race Headquarters, and described the overall situation as best I could. As I had expected he would, Mark offered to come to my aid, suggesting that one of his longer spinnaker poles might be of use to me if I decided not to abandon ship. Thanking him profusely, I refused, knowing full well that accepting outside assistance of any kind while under way would result in my automatic disqualification from the race. I assured him that I was physically okay, but would need time to devise and construct a proper jury-rig for the boat. I spoke also to Hal Roth, Pentti Salmi, and David White (an American sailing the Class-One boat *Legend Securities*), all of whom made open offers of assistance. Difficult though it was, I had to decline. Agreeing to make contact again in two hours' time, I signed off.

The silence that followed talking with friends, drawing strength from their concern, was overwhelming. I found myself close to tears, not for myself and my situation (although I'm sure the after-effects of the shock had something to do with it), but for the camaraderie that was almost tangible over the airwaves. Pulling myself together, I tried to concentrate on the matter at hand. The violent motion of the boat was making the smallest of tasks seem Herculean; what I needed was some sail up, even if it was only temporary. Making my way carefully up to the bow on all fours, I dug the storm jib out of the sail locker and set about hoisting it on the "radio mast." Although grossly inefficient as a means of propulsion, when this sail was finally set an hour later, it did wonders in steadying the boat.

Down below, I put on another pot of coffee and spent the next hour cleaning up and pumping out the overflowing bilges. Tidying up always helped raise my spirits, and by the time ten o'clock rolled around and it was time for the radio again, I was feeling much better about things. I still hadn't had time to put a great deal of thought into a proper rig, or into where I should head once it was built, but two things seemed quite clear to me: first, however I utilized the two spinnaker poles to fashion a mast, it would have to be strong. In these latitudes, I could expect heavy gales, and if I lost the new mast overboard, my chances of survival would go with it. Second, to steer westward back towards New Zealand, the closest piece of land, was out of the question. To do so would be to head against the current and the prevailing winds, an impossible task under jury-rig. Discussing these points with Mark and the others helped tremendously. Based on the experiences of Hal Roth and Bertie Reed, I elected as my destination the Chilean port of Talcahuano, some 3,500 miles to the north-east. I still hadn't looked at a chart, but I would have to make a landfall on the west coast of South America, and Talcahuano was ostensibly the southernmost port with the proper facilities. Ideas for the jury-rig came in thick and fast, and what I eventually decided upon was a hybrid of my own thinking and the suggestions of the others.

The rest of the afternoon and early evening I worked hard straightening up the boat and laying the groundwork for the new rig. Several hours were spent with pencil and paper, drawing diagrams and making notes. I tried to think through every phase of the operation, determined to get it right the first time — mistakes would be costly. Ideas were modified or discarded altogether, depending upon the availability of suitable bits and pieces with which to do the job. By nightfall I was cold, hungry, and very tired, but the preliminary work had been finished. After a quick "boil-in-the-bag" meal and a cup of tea, I crawled into the damp quarterberth and, setting the alarm to wake me shortly before dawn, I quickly fell asleep.

In the morning, sipping coffee in the darkness, I waited for first light to make working on deck a little easier. I began by taking down yesterday's temporary rig. The weather was co-operating, with the wind staying light from the south-east, although I paid a penalty in having to endure a steady cold rain. Within an hour I was ready to begin in earnest.

I had decided to use the two spinnaker poles to construct an A-frame "mast," to build it flat on the deck, and then to raise it into position. Moving carefully, I secured the bottom ends of the two spinnaker poles to toggles on the chainplates, using large hoseclamps. Pads made from plywood and flattened coffee cans were fastened to the deck just inboard of the chainplates. These would prevent the poles from chafing against the deck once they were erect. Forward, I brought the ends of the poles together and lashed them solidly with more hoseclamps and lengths of rope. To this new "masthead" I attached four blocks with halyards rove through them. The radio antenna, insulated once again with rubber and electrical tape, was led through one of the pole ends. For rigging, two ropes were led from aft using the same set-up as the original running backstays and tied firmly to the apex of the A-frame. The tails of these two stays I then brought right forward, after leading them through the blocks on the stern. The forestay I fashioned from one of the fifteen-foot wire jackstays, with the old boom-vang tackle on the bottom end attaching it to the stemhead. This was set approximately to the length that would be required when the rig was vertical. A fourth line was led from the head of the A-frame down through a block at the old mast collar, and back to a winch. This would serve to keep the whole rig firmly pulled down against the deck. Finally, a number of lashings were added between the two legs of the bipod for additional strength.

The whole process took about four hours, until I was ready to raise the jury-rigged mast into position. Squatting up on the bow, I lifted the head of the A-frame a few feet and set it on my shoulders. Holding the tails of the running backstays like a pair

117

of reins, I slowly stood up. Moving gradually aft, I used one hand now to push the rig ever closer to the vertical, all the while keeping tension on the backstays. Suddenly, as the bow of the boat rose on a swell, the A-frame tottered backwards! Heart in my mouth, I frantically took up the slack in the backstays. With a crash, the forestay came tight and held. The jury-rig was up, albeit leaning about ten degrees aft of the vertical. Crawling back and forth between the bow and stern, I adjusted the tension on the stays until the A-frame was upright. Over the course of the next hour I went over the set-up with a critical eye, adding lashings where needed, making sure that nothing was left to chance. Once I was satisfied, I slipped below for a well-deserved coffee and a bite to eat.

Anxious to get underway, I was soon back on deck. All I needed now were sails. For the "mainsail," I had decided to use the storm trisail. Although made of very heavy cloth, it was closest to the shape I needed and I was loath to chop up any of the headsails for the job; I would need them later. After some experimentation, I finally had my mainsail up and drawing, a rope strop shortening it to the correct height. For the jib, one of the two #4s was pressed into service. Hoisted on the forestay, also with a strop to shorten it to the correct height, it seemed to set quite well.

It had been almost thirty-two hours since the dismasting, and a much-modified *Joseph Young* was underway once more.

February 9, 1987
49 45S 147 00W

Three days since disaster struck. The last twenty-four hours have been pure hell, completely destroying the sense of accomplishment I felt after setting up the jury-rig. The light wind, which made conditions easier initially, has died away completely. In its wake I have been left with the most confused swell I've ever seen. Under a low overcast, rain is falling almost continuously. The sea is black and cold, and twenty-foot swells are coming from every direction. Joseph Young *is being thrown around like a cork, making cooking impossible. I have fallen more times than I can count and am covered in bruises as a result. The motion of the boat is positively wicked.*

On the bright side, I actually managed to get a phone call home to Vicki via Sydney Radio last night. I was quite surprised that the makeshift antenna worked as well as it did, though I had to pick the time and frequency with care. Hearing her voice after the events of the last few days was a real tonic (despite the fact that I cried for an hour after the call). Through the chat hour, the rest of the guys are being very supportive. Jean-Luc is organizing a lobby with the other French competitors to try to get me a replacement mast from France at no cost. Bertie is doing the same thing through his contacts at home. Mike Plant on Airco Distributor, *a Class-Two American yacht, has offered some cash, and Hal Roth is making some calls for me. I couldn't have had a better crew.*

By afternoon today, we finally got some wind. South-east at Force 5 — not the best direction but at least I'm moving, doing 6 knots, which is amazing. The improvement in the boat's motion with some wind to steady the sails is unbelievable. Although I need to head east, not north-north-east, I can now gauge the speed potential given favourable winds, which is encouraging. I simply have to reach *Newport in time for the prize-giving on May 30.*

By the following morning the wind had dropped off again, leaving me frustrated and uncomfortable. Two things have become

119

crystal clear over the last twelve hours. First, with the small amount of sail I am able to hoist, any wind of less than 10 knots is as good as being becalmed. Second, *Joseph Young* is now sailing like a square-rigger, unable to point closer than eighty degrees to the wind. I am now more than ever dependent upon favourable winds to see me safely to land.

There were a couple of bright spots in that otherwise miserable day. I was listening to the radio broadcast early in the morning, when two New Zealand operators came on with a message for me. Mac (ZL4JG) and Ron (ZL4MK) had obtained permission for me to converse with them through the amateur ham-radio network. Although I didn't have the proper licence, extenuating circumstances had prompted the New Zealand authorities to issue me a dispensation. This was a real godsend, as I was sure to lose all other contact with the outside world once the rest of the competitors had rounded the Horn. To know that I would always have someone (anyone!) to talk to in the weeks ahead was a real boost. Also, just before noon, I found another hidden card from Vicki. I had opened up the aft food locker for the first time since I had left Sydney, in search of some Ovaltine, and there, on top of the cans and crates, was an envelope. Picking it up, I laid it reverently on the chart table. I contemplated it like a child looking under the tree on Christmas morning, my heart thumping with anticipation. Savouring the moment, I let it sit unopened while I made a cup of tea and put some music on the tape deck. When the time was right, I finally looked inside the envelope.

1630: wind finally shifted a bit more to the south. Making a course of 045 degrees true, but terribly uncomfortable. Crawled into wet sleeping bag for half an hour to warm up. Bag smells awful! Felt better afterwards though, and had one of the Finnish boil-in-the-bag meals and a cup of tea for supper.

1700: Reported my position through the ham-radio network. Heard that Pentti (Colt by Rettig) will be stopping in the Falkland Islands with rudder problems. Bailed out the space forward of the mast. Bilge almost full again. Read Vicki's card once more. I will *survive. Too much living to do yet.*

By nightfall the wind had gone back to the east and reached full gale force. It lasted like this for just over two days. In an area renowned for its westerly breeze, this was particularly frustrating. At the height of the gale, I was forced to take down the jib after several of the hanks securing it to the forestay tore through the sailcloth. Progress was pitiful. Since being dismasted I had moved a scant 129 miles closer to Talcahuano. At this rate it would be almost six months before I reached land. By then, of course, I would long be dead of thirst and/or starvation. Something was going to have to change.

February 14, 1987
45 29S 142 34W

0900: wind southerly at last! Even a few patches of sunshine above. Managed to take apart the patch on the deck and reassemble it using the last tube of caulking. With any luck it will no longer leak, or at least not as badly as before. Life will be a lot easier without those gallons of water sloshing around down below. Spoke to Bertie Reed on the 0730 radio schedule, which was good.

2100: feeling quite okay tonight. Supper was so good I was smiling (didn't realize how hungry I was). Kippers and toast followed by a can of brie and crackers. Sitting here with a hot rum toddy listening to Joe Cocker on the tape deck. So far the wind is holding.

February 15, 1987
45 05S 139 52W

Evening: a good day's sailing at last, covered 115 miles noon to noon. Sent a message to Race Committee Chairman Robin Knox-Johnston via radio this morning; ''Stopping Talcahuano, Chile, for spare parts. Estimated time of arrival March 20. Estimated time of

departure March 27. No intention of withdrawing. Please consider
waiving Rule 3.3 regarding Rio. What date final cricket match of
tour, Newport? Regards, Master, Joseph Young." Hung up the
sleeping bag in the cabin this afternoon to try and dry it a bit. Felt
really grubby—boiled two kettles of water and had a shampoo,
sponge bath, and a shave. Put on clean clothes. Feels great! Cooked a
cheese omelette and rice for supper. Lots of eggs left, and they will all
need eating soon.

Spoke with Mark and Hal on the evening chat hour.

I had sent an official message to Robin for several reasons.
Under the race rules, I was required to indicate my intention to
make an unscheduled stop. My main worry, however, was that
the committee would ask me to withdraw. This they could
legally do if I arrived in Rio more than thirty days after the first
boat in Class Two. Completing the race within the context of the
rules, and in time for the final ceremonies in Newport, was
becoming a driving ambition with me. I have always hated to
leave anything unfinished. When I had voiced my concern
about being disqualified to the other boats, their show of soli-
darity had touched me deeply. All of them had said that if push
came to shove, they would all withdraw too.

February 16, 1987
44 42S 137 34W

0830: up late last night to call Vicki. Managed to get through on 12
Mhz with Sydney Radio; a good copy on them but hard for Vicki to
hear me. The call depressed me more than anything else, but nice to
hear her voice. Woke up this morning to virtual calm; barometer way
up, and a high, long swell from the south.

1930: totally becalmed since 0900 this morning. I just can't believe
this crap! Dismasted ten days ago and since then I've had about forty
hours of fair winds—that is anything over 10 knots between north
and south-through-west. I am seething with barely controlled anger.
Not even a bird or dolphin to break the spell; the weather still totally
overcast. Sitting here, Joseph Young lurching all over the place, I

*am very depressed. Turned off the electronic log; too soul-destroying
to see it registering 0 knots for speed.*

*Tried flying a spinnaker this morning but it was useless. Just not
enough height on the bipod. To keep busy, I took up the floorboards
and cleaned around the battery locker and reprogrammed all channels
in the single-sideband radio. Also rewired a second buzzer to the log
alarm.*

*Spoke with Mark on the evening chat hour and received a
message from Robin Knox-Johnston: "Every consideration will be
given to extending Rule 14.1 of the Sailing Instructions. However,
Rule 3.3 must apply. All assistance will be requested in Rio for a fast
turnaround. Looking forward to your presence at the final match of
the tournament. Good luck and fair winds. RKJ."*

February 17, 1987
44 33S 137 01W

*Remained becalmed all day. Spent three hours cleaning: stove, sink,
woodwork, scrubbed deckhead (filthy!), polished barometer, teak-oiled
tiller—all to keep busy. Don't feel bad today really. Have accepted
my lot—for now. Much warmer and some sunshine, which has
helped. Had my shirt off for much of the day. Hung the sleeping bag
on deck to dry it out a bit, but it really needs to be burnt.*

February 18, 1987
44 40S 136 54W

*No wind—still. Had a few hours of light east-north-east breeze, so
took down the #4 and tailored the drifter for the new "mast." Ate
the last bit of bacon for breakfast this morning, made pancakes for
lunch, and kippers for supper. A little nude sunbathing on deck this
morning reading Marlowe's* Edward II.

February 20, 1987
46 14S 135 02W

*Light north-easterly wind from yesterday is still with me. So sick
with frustration. At this abysmal rate I will be lucky to make* land

*alive, never mind the Newport prize-giving. Two weeks now since
the disaster and not a breath of favourable wind. Read* Hamlet *and*
The Tempest *yesterday. Removed damaged lifelines and runner
tails, also took in the spinnaker guys and sheets. The boat is so stiff
without the mast, that even in the very short chop (three-to-four-foot
seas) the motion is whip-like. Great fun.*

February 21, 1987
46 44S 134 14W

*Wind from the east and light. Up at 0200 and tried tacking. Ran to
the north for four hours, then tacked again in frustration. A course
to the south-south-east has simply got to be better.*

*Have just about decided to go round the Horn to the Falkland
Islands rather than to Chile, but will see what the weather does in
the next week before committing myself. However, in this present
weather pattern I have no chance of making Talcahuano before I
either die of thirst or go mad. The advantages of going directly to the
Falklands are:*
1 *the mileage from here to Chile and to the Falklands is identical,*
2 *it will be easier to deal with the British than with the Chileans,*
3 *after rerigging the boat, I will be closer to Rio by 2,100 miles.*

*The only drawback is the danger of rough weather, and not
knowing how* Joseph Young *will handle it.*

Over the course of that week depression had settled over me
like a lead blanket. I had bottomed on February 21 with the news
that the last of the other boats had rounded Cape Horn. I now
felt truly alone, the nearest land still 3,000 miles over the horizon. More and more, the idea of not succeeding ate at me. I
questioned whether I would be able to live with myself if I let
this very personal goal slip through my fingers. Once it was
gone, no matter what I did in the future, I would never be able
to grasp it again. To the north lay calmer weather, safety, and
almost certain failure. Even if I was able to reach Talcahuano
without outside assistance in the form of food and water, my
chances of sailing from there, down around Cape Horn, and

back to Newport in time for the finish were now virtually nil. To the south lay some of the roughest ocean in the world, Cape Horn, the Falklands, and my only chance to succeed. I had reached the wall, and had to decide whether to skirt around it, or go over the top.

February 22, 1987
47 32S 134 33W

So—becalmed all last night and still no wind this morning. Weather overcast and cool. The more I think about heading for Port Stanley in the Falklands, the better I like it. I should never have listened to the others, or I should have listened but believed in myself. When I initially suggested carrying on for the Horn the day after being dismasted, they all decried the idea. I would now be much closer to my final destination if I had stayed south. A joke really; the guys were putting forward Tahiti and New Zealand as possible destinations! In fact, I think I am safe enough down here. The Roaring Forties? More like the Snoring Forties.

Can't help thinking how much easier it would have been to have been killed outright rather than to have suffered this frustration. My rage is just barely controlled; am wondering how one knows when insanity finally sets in.

February 24, 1987
48 32S 131 57W

Bored to death! I came for the sailing, and now that that's been done away with there's not much left. I've read all of the books on board, some of them twice. Had a terrible night; felt very ill and could not sleep properly. Must have been something I ate. I've been thinking more about the Port Stanley vs. Talcahuano argument. Looking through my charts, I have the latest one covering the Falklands, but nothing for Chile. I feel that the danger of going aground near Talcahuano is quite large. The whole coast is virtually a lee shore, and with this jury-rig I can't sail to weather worth a damn.

February 25 marked my thirty-eighth day at sea; half of those days had been spent without a mast. I dragged myself out of the bunk shortly before sunrise, to discover that nothing much had changed. The wind (if it could be called such) was half-heartedly moving *Joseph Young* along at barely 2 knots. It was another cold, damp, overcast day with frequent drizzle. After breakfast, I decided to take the weekly whether-I-needed-it-or-not bath. Boiling a kettle, I stripped off and shivered for half an hour while I shampooed, shaved, and sponged. Pulling on a clean set of clothes I felt much revived. A little concerned about using fresh water for anything other than drinking, I resolved to try to catch a litre or two if it started to rain in earnest.

After tidying up a little down below, I sat down with pencil, paper, and chart to work out some accurate distances to a land-fall. After some fairly simple calculations, I determined that I was now 2,313 miles from Cape Horn, and 2,632 miles from Talcahuano. From my figures, this meant that I had managed a rather pathetic 57 miles a day at an average speed of 2.4 knots since the dismasting. Not exactly encouraging. Something was going to have to change.

That evening, I tuned in to the chat hour as usual, despite the fact that I hadn't been able to contact any of the other boats for over a week now. Much to my surprise, I heard Hal faintly in the background. Quickly putting out a call, I managed to arrange another one for an hour from now, when perhaps the reception would be a little better. Trying not to get my hopes up, I none the less charged the batteries and made coffee as I waited for the minutes to tick away.

At 1900 hours I switched the radio on again, praying for a change in my luck. Right on cue, Hal's voice cut through the static and boomed out of the loudspeaker. I felt as if I had returned to the land of the living. After catching up on news of the others (the first two boats had already arrived in Rio) I steered the conversation towards my predicament. Calmly I explained my thoughts about Cape Horn and the Falklands to Hal, putting forward all the rational arguments I could muster. In my mind, I was desperately seeking some form of tacit sup-port. If worst came to worst, I didn't want to be remembered as

126

a foolhardy amateur. I certainly wasn't expecting outright encouragement, but the negative reaction I received stunned me. Pentti Salmi had been in on the conversation and he came straight out vehemently against the idea. "The heroes I know are all dead," was how he put it. Mark was listening too, although I couldn't hear him, and through Hal he voiced his opposition as well. Hal wasn't entirely enthusiastic either, though he did suggest some alternatives.

The concern that my friends, all of them with thousands of sailing miles behind them, showed was based on their fears for my safety. However, as I noted in my journal, they're not in my shoes, and whatever they say, don't know what I'm going through. I am sure that if the situation was reversed, I would feel the same way that they do. Still, at the moment their contributions have served mainly to make me aware that I am very much alone out here, and I must be alone in reaching my decision. I hope that they will be able to understand.

That evening as I lay down to sleep my mind was greatly troubled with thoughts of the month ahead of me. I woke in the middle of the night, coming to with a start, bathed in sweat. I lay there in the coffin-like confines of the quarterberth, really frightened for the first time in many days. Getting up, I poked my head out through the hatch and gazed around in the darkness. The solitude was crushing me; it was hard to believe that land, and other people, really did exist out there beyond the horizon.

For the next two days the wind remained very light from the north. That I managed to cover 116 miles was due in no small way to the current, which was carrying us steadily eastward. At noon on February 27 I crossed the fiftieth parallel of latitude. The latest weather map still showed a large high-pressure system sitting to the north and east of my position. In the log-book that day, for the first time since losing the mast, I recorded only one distance under the space labelled "distance to go": 2,197 miles to Cape Horn. Come what may, I had decided, I was going to the Falkland Islands. There would be no turning back.

Finally, unbelievably, on February 28, I found some favourable winds. The northerly breeze that had started to fill in the previous evening had strengthened to a good Force 5 by morning, and *Joseph Young* was rolling along at the amazing speed of 5 knots. This was more like it. If I could average a hundred miles a day, we could be in port in a mere four weeks. The very thought of it made everything seem so much easier to bear.

Making breakfast that morning I was suddenly struck by how much my ideas of comfort and discomfort had changed over the past year. I wondered what people would say if they could see me now. Looking around, I began to laugh. Every inch of the interior woodwork, damp and cold since the mast had broken through the deck, was now a gentle shade of green, coloured by the rapidly growing mould. In contrast, black mildew was spreading unchecked over the previously white deckhead and sides. Tiny rivulets of water, from the still-leaking chainplate, chased each other around on the workbench before finding their way onto the cabin sole. Luxury now was a damp — as opposed to a soggy — sleeping bag. In the frying pan, the best meal of the day was almost ready to eat. The allotted two slices of soured black bread, the worst of the mould trimmed from the edges, were frying up nicely. From the almost totally depleted supply of eggs I chose the worst-looking one of the bunch, and, after scraping the green fuzz from the shell, cracked it into a cup. The yoke was a little black even for my taste, so it had to be tossed overboard. The second one I tried was fine, however, only slightly dark, barely noticeable after it was scrambled. At home, the whole mess would have gone in the garbage — out here it was absolutely delicious!

The northerly wind that I welcomed that morning was in fact the precursor of three days of utter misery, during which *Joseph Young* and I hung on by the skin of our teeth. A small depression developed quickly and passed to the north of us, bringing gale-force head winds and tremendous seas.

March 1, 1987
52 43S 124 45W

Weather is terrible. The worst seas of this leg to date. Wind was from the east at 40 knots this morning, and has now shifted to the south-east. Was forced to take down the headsail in an effort to keep the bow towards the sea. The boat is being tossed sideways by every wave, dropping heavily into the troughs. All battened down below; clammy, damp, and miserable. Much to my surprise I was able to get a phone call through to Vicki this morning, which really helped. Hope I didn't sound too down to her, but I am so depressed.

March 2, 1987
52 08S 123 27W

Gale still continues with the wind from the south-east. A large wave in the middle of the night spun Joseph Young *around so far the sails were taken aback. Struggled up on deck to sort things out. Really blowing now, very cold, bad seas. Don't know how we haven't been rolled right over. Boat taking an awful beating. Could only manage toast and coffee for breakfast. Everything soaking wet down below again.*

March 4, 1987
51 31S 118 36W

The wind is now out of the south at last so we are making some miles, though still grossly uncomfortable. The satellite navigator stopped working last night. Checked with the meter and it seems to be the same problem as before. I hope I can effect temporary repair when the weather becomes more favourable. What will go wrong next? This ocean is real torture!I tallied up the winds since the dismasting. Twenty-two out of twenty-seven days the wind has been calm or contrary. Prevailing westerlies?

Had a curry for supper, first proper meal in three days — excellent, but an infection in my left ear is quite painful and makes chewing difficult.

March 6, 1987
51 48S 114 30W

*Ran out of bread yesterday. Tried making porridge for breakfast —
probably better as a caulking compound than as food, but ate most of
it. Wind is westerly this morning, which is wonderful. Just praying
it holds for three weeks. Managed to partially repair the satellite
navigator today, which is a help.*

On the afternoon of March 6, a moderate westerly wind materialized, leading me to believe that I had finally escaped the
clutches of the high-pressure weather system. However, I was
wakened at 0500 the next morning by the lack of wind and by
Joseph Young rolling sickeningly in the long swell. The next forty
hours were the most difficult, mentally, that I have ever faced.

It seemed that absolutely everything was working against
me. The weather was taunting me, raising my hopes with short
bursts of favourable wind, only to dash them again with calms
or head winds. The frustration I felt is indescribable. To add to
my woes, the satellite navigator still refused to work, and I
remained unable to receive weather maps to give me even a
furtive glimpse at what lay ahead. With no heat on the boat, and
the temperature falling closer and closer to zero each night,
drying out was next to impossible. Simply staying warm had
become a struggle.

To try and keep my mind from dwelling on the present, I
worked on odd jobs around the boat, going over the satellite
navigator yet again, covering the patch on deck with self-adhe-
sive sailcloth, and cleaning up as best I could. I drew strength
from the trials of others, thinking in particular of the tenacity
and endurance that Shackleton had shown under conditions
much worse than my own during his ill-fated expedition to the
South Pole. Pulling out the few pictures I had with me of my
grandfather, Joseph Young, I knew that he would not have
approved of my self-pity. I would just have to accept my lot as
it was dealt to me. Tomorrow was, after all, another day.

At 0200 on March 9, I drifted out of a deep sleep, responding to a definite change in the motion of the boat. When I had climbed into the bunk four hours earlier, the wind had been light and from the west-north-west. Listening to it now, it was obvious that it had increased substantially; I could hear it shrieking in the rigging. Cursing, I donned boots, sweater, and oilskins before sliding back the hatch. I was met by an icy blast, and, clipping on the safety harness, pulled myself up into the cockpit. As my eyes adjusted to the darkness I took stock of the situation. The wind was bitterly cold, blowing a good 50 knots. The drifter, which was still hoisted forward, had to come down. Moving groggily, still half asleep, I let the sheet off and crawled forward. Sitting on the foredeck I struggled for the next twenty minutes to wrestle the sail down, my hands numbed by the wind and water. Packing it in the sailbag was out of the question, so I simply stuffed the works down the forehatch. I dragged the #4 up, and took another half an hour setting it, and by the time I regained the shelter of the cabin I was half frozen. A quick cup of tea helped me warm up a little before I wormed my way back into my damp, chilly bunk. This wind was just what we needed if we were to make some miles, and I fell asleep willing it to hold.

Throughout the remainder of that day the wind continued unabated, soon building the seas up to an impressive height. *Joseph Young* seemed more than able to handle it though, and romped along, our speed never dipping below 5 knots. Such progress was the best thing that could have happened as far as my morale went, and that night, for the first time in weeks, I turned in feeling content. The falling barometer told me that the wind should last for some time to come.

The next morning a novel sight greeted me when I ventured on deck. Piled in the corners of the cockpit were snowdrifts. In disbelief I reached out and scooped some into my hand. More hail than snow perhaps, but winter was obviously just around the corner. It never occurred to me at this time that I was holding in my hand a very precious commodity—a source of fresh water. I only thought enviously of the other competitors, most by now basking on the beaches in Rio. With over twelve hundred miles still to go before Cape Horn, it would be a while yet before I could start heading north. I hoped it wasn't going to get too much colder.

March 12, 1987
54 41S 96 37W

This morning I received the biggest fright sea conditions have ever given me. I think I am quite lucky to still be in one piece. After getting up at about 0600, I spent nearly an hour on deck checking over the jury-rig and sails. The swell was very high after the continuous gale-force winds of the last three days, but we seemed to be riding it out quite nicely, averaging over 5 knots in the following sea. Down below again, I put some music on and began frying some corned beef for breakfast. I opened the hatch above me about six inches to vent out the cooking fumes. About five minutes later I heard a faint hissing and rumbling noise, and thought that the cassette I was listening to must be on its last legs. A few seconds later I realized the noise was getting much louder all the time, so I glanced up through the slightly open hatch (the line-of-sight here being about fifty degrees above the horizontal). What I saw stopped me cold. Towering perhaps twenty feet directly over the stern of the boat was an absolutely sheer wall of water! Sections of the already breaking crest were tumbling down the face of the wave like little waterfalls, white streaks of froth against a grey background. Stark terror goading me into action, I reached up with both hands and slammed the hatch. The hatch slid past the stops and jammed, leaving a three-inch gap at its forward end—adrenalin had given me strength I never knew I had. I was still struggling to free it when the wave crashed down upon us. The force of the impact staggered me, and as I reeled across the cabin, water poured in through the partially open hatch with the pressure of a fire hose, knocking me flat. The noise was simply incredible; I wondered if we were going down. Eyes fixed upon the hatch, I dragged myself up, but had barely gained my feet when we were struck the second time. My world became a nightmare of noise and confusion as Joseph Young *was thrown sideways and rolled. Landing heavily on the settee, I*

shielded my head as tools, books, and anything else that wasn't
bolted down flew across the cabin. Once again, Joseph Young
recovered, and as things settled down I was finally able to reach the
hatch and wrest it free. Clamping it shut I gripped the ladder and
braced myself, waiting for the killer. Through all this insanity, the
tape deck played away undisturbed, adding a macabre touch to this
scene of destruction. Around me, water ran freely from the flooded
drawers and lockers. The bilges full, I stood ankle-deep in a sea of
garbage, breakfast, books, kitchen utensils, and items of every
description washing back and forth across the cabin sole. I prayed,
without much hope, that the jury-rig had come through intact.
Soaked to the skin, shivering from cold and shock, I remained frozen
in anticipation of the next wave for a full five minutes. Nothing.
Talking loudly to myself for encouragement, I mustered up the
courage to cautiously slide open the hatch and pop my head out for a
look around. Amazingly, the mast was still in place, although the
sails had suffered. The dodger around the hatch was torn completely
away from its track, and ropes were trailing in the water alongside.
The sea looked no worse than it had done first thing this morning.
Encouraged, I ventured out into the cockpit to man the pumps. I
ticked off another of my nine lives.

March 13, 1987
54 29S 92 36W

The port drinking-water tank ran dry this afternoon. Should be an
ample supply in the starboard tank, though without gauges it is a
little worrying. Sea water is still pouring in by the chainplates.
Every available towel and rag is laid out on the workbench to try and
stem the flood. So miserably wet down below it's almost unbearable
— except that I have to bear it. A warm, dry, bed ashore is the stuff
my dreams are made of.

Progress is good though; covered 140 miles in the last twenty-
four hours. With only 870 miles to go before reaching Cape Horn, I
should be able to make it in a week even if the wind drops off a bit.
The sooner the better, it has become quite the mental barrier. I am
getting tired of this feeling of apprehension I have about it.

133

March 14, 1987
54 38S 88 20W

Continued good progress with westerly gale-force winds. Made 148 miles today at an average speed of 6.2 knots. Very rough sea and high swell. Had to re-attach the headsail to the forestay again today with plastic cable ties. The uneven strain on the sail is tearing the hanks away from the cloth.

March 15, 1987
54 26S 84 22W

Today my situation took a surprising turn for the worse. When I attempted to make a cup of tea this afternoon the starboard fresh-water tank came up empty. It took a minute for the implications to sink in, but potentially this could be very bad news. From the survival kit I retrieved two five-litre plastic bottles of water; it certainly doesn't look like much.

I managed to make contact with one of the radio operators in the evening, and after phoning a local doctor he passed along the information that I would require a minimum of one litre of water a day to survive. With 590 miles between Joseph Young and Cape Horn, and 1,100 miles in total to the Falklands, I should be all right as long as the wind remains favourable. I will no longer be able to use fresh water for cooking. Worse, I must ration my intake of hot drinks, the only source of heat my body has at the moment. Life, surely, cannot get anything but better from here on in.

March 16, 1987
55 20S 81 07W

Had a real stroke of luck today for the first time in a long while. I woke just before dawn to the sound of hail beating on the deck. Up on deck I dashed like a man possessed, wielding a saucepan in either hand. I managed to fill both pots, and, melted, that amounts to almost another whole litre of only slightly salty water. Luxury! After some deliberation, I treated myself to half a cup of coffee and bannock or pan bread for breakfast. I mixed flour, water, and baking soda in a

bowl, and gently fried the resulting dough. Eaten hot, dripping with
margarine and marmalade, it was like manna from heaven. A nice
change from corned beef and crackers. After breakfast I crawled back
in the sleeping bag until noon; it's the only place I can stay warm.
It's been very cold for the last day or two.

Three days later, *Joseph Young* and I were finally within striking
distance of the Horn. Not having been able to fix my position
for almost twenty-four hours, I was nervous about being so close
to land, and spent the entire day on deck, peering through the
drizzle and mist. I wished I had a bit more room between myself
and the coast, for if the wind shifted round to the south we could
find ourselves on a lee shore. By my best estimate, we were
ninety-five miles from Cabo de Hornos itself, and should sight
land before nightfall. I could notice a distinct change in the sea
from twelve hours ago. The waves now were much steeper and
breaking more frequently, the result of the decreasing water
depth. The hours passed with excruciating slowness, the
motion of the boat worse than ever. At three-thirty in the afternoon the drizzle eased a bit, and out of the murk to the north
appeared a black, squat lump, just visible on the horizon. A
shiver ran through me. This, truly, was the bottom of the world.
Binoculars and chart helped confirm that I was looking at Islas
Alfonso, and from here I set a course to take me a little farther
south and clear of the Horn.

In the journal later that night I wrote: *Well, saw land for the*
first time in over sixty days, passing a couple of miles south of Islas
Alfonso. Will round the Horn itself during the hours of darkness, but
am not really disappointed that I won't actually see it. Better to go fast
and get off the continental shelf before something nasty happens. The
seas are very steep, high, and breaking.

At 2000 hours I lay down to try and get some rest. The quarterberth was still wringing wet from the flood of a week ago, so
I settled myself, fully clothed, on the settee and lashed myself
in. No sooner had I fallen asleep than all hell broke loose.
Instantly awake, I had the sensation of falling through the darkness. A noise like a train in a tunnel filled my ears. A second

later *Joseph Young* was slammed with unbelievable violence, the impact resembling that of a bad car crash. The shock knocked the wind from my chest. I was pinned against the ropes holding me in the berth as *Joseph Young* rolled beneath me. In the absolute blackness of the cabin, tools and spare parts rained down on me from the workbench opposite. Through all this chaos I heard the faint sound of breaking glass. It registered in my mind that with the hatch stove in, we were finished. It all seemed such a waste.

Before I could gather my thoughts, I was pressed against the back of the settee as the yacht spun in the opposite direction. Completely disorientated, I grappled for the handrail above me, willing this nightmare to end one way or the other. Suddenly, as quickly as it had begun, the noise and the insane motion stopped. Not wasting a moment, I clawed at the ropes holding me in and swung out of the bunk. Throwing back the hatch, which, surprisingly, was still intact, I scurried up on deck, not knowing what to expect.

With relief I noted that the jury-rig was still standing. I steered the boat back on course and reset the auto-pilot. The jib was flogging badly and needed my attention, the halyard having been carried away and most of the hanks as well. The mainsail, fortunately, appeared undamaged, though slack, and gave enough speed for control. The waves were still huge, but didn't seem any more dangerous than they had been yesterday. An hour's hard work had the deck back in order and the sails trimmed, so I returned below to face the mess there. As I gazed around I felt tired and deflated. Just as I thought I was winning, the ocean would deal me another blow to drag me right back down again. With a sigh of resignation I set about cleaning up. Sleep was out of the question.

It was difficult to determine exactly what had happened during those few minutes of fear, noise, and confusion, but I believe *Joseph Young* was overtaken by a particularly steep, high wave; one that overpowered the auto-pilot and caused the boat to broach until broadside to the seas. The sensation I had of falling was so acute, that I feel the crest of the wave literally threw *Joseph*

Young forward, to land heavily on her side in the trough of the swell, where she then rolled down past the horizontal. The sound of breaking glass was, in fact, caused by bottles of chutney and relish shattering against the inside of the boat after flying across the cabin. That *Joseph Young* survived with no structural damage is a testament to the strength of her construction. It was very fortunate that I was securely strapped in the bunk at the time.

It was almost dawn before I had the cabin back in some semblance of order. The floorboards I retrieved from the heads, where they had lodged themselves after flying around the boat. Chutney was smeared across the deckhead and the desk opposite the galley. From the bilges I scooped out tea bags, cutlery, and tools. Finally everything was stowed back in place, and I turned my thoughts to breakfast. During the last few hours, we had actually rounded the Horn, the most famous landmark to sailors everywhere. And I had been busy with housework!

Since leaving Sydney, I had been hoarding a special treat especially to mark this occasion — a Christmas pudding complete with rum-butter sauce. Warmed in a saucepan, and washed down with half a cup of tea, it was just the thing for a celebratory breakfast. I offered a silent thank you to *Joseph Young*, battered but not beaten, for seeing me through safely thus far.

When mid-morning came, I altered course towards the north-east and the Falkland Islands. Only four hundred miles left to go. With Cape Horn astern of us at long last, I truly felt that we had "rounded the corner" and left the worst behind. It had been an awfully long two months.

On March 22 I made my best-ever run under jury-rig, 157 miles noon-to-noon at a speed of 6.8 knots. The wind had been south-west ever since we had cleared the Horn, exactly the direction I needed, and always blowing at gale force too. Radio contact had been established with the Royal Navy in the Falklands, due mainly to the efforts of James Hatfield, a British yachtsman with whom I had spoken on the radio. It sounded like they were ready to receive me in fine style. In fact, the day before, I had had to quell their enthusiasm for my cause a little.

Knowing that I was dangerously short of water, they had arranged for an aircraft to fly over and drop supplies to me at sea. This, of course, would have disqualified me from the race, but I had a hard time persuading them that I was okay. I got the impression that they were quite disappointed, so anxious were they to help.

With only ninety miles to go at noon, I began planning my approach carefully. A mistake at this stage would be disastrous. With the satellite navigator still not working properly, I resolved to make a landfall first off Beauchêne Island, which lay approximately fifty miles from the harbour entrance. This would give me a definite position from which to work. Fortunately, the visibility was good, and at exactly 1500 hours the island came into view off the port bow. So far, so good. Sailing about ten miles past this rocky pinnacle, I turned and hove to. It was essential that I didn't close with the coast under darkness, as the risk of running ashore was simply too great. Lighthouses did not exist in this part of the world. It was hard to believe that within twelve hours my ordeal would be over. My nerves were stretched taut as piano wires with anticipation. I couldn't sleep for excitement, so spent the next eight hours giving the boat one last clean, rigging the anchor, and having a salt-water shampoo and shave.

At one o'clock in the morning I hoisted the jib for the last time and pointed *Joseph Young*'s bow towards the north. By my best calculations, dawn should find me two miles off the coast, within sight of land. From now on, I could not leave the deck.

As the first early light of dawn crept across the eastern sky, I strained my eyes ahead, willing the dark mass of land to show itself. Patches of drifting kelp floated by, doing little to put my mind at ease. Suddenly, in the greyness ahead, I saw a faint, broken, white line. Puzzled, heart pounding, I watched it for a minute. All at once I realized what that white line must be, and with a shout of panic I leapt for the tiller. What I was seeing were breakers on the shore. The very low, featureless land that was the Falklands was nearly invisible against the overcast sky. Putting *Joseph Young* onto an easterly course, I dashed below to pore over the chart. Unless my dead reckoning was way off, I had to be cruising up the coast of Lively Island. The entrance to Mares' Harbour, therefore, lay two miles farther east. I called HMS *Dunbarton Castle*, and the Royal Navy confirmed that they were on their way out to meet me. Back on deck, I guided *Joseph Young* up the coast, dodging ugly swathes of kelp. Within half an hour HMS *Dunbarton Castle* steamed into sight and proceeded ahead of me to take up a position two miles from the dock, marking the point at which I could accept a tow within the context of the race rules.

At 1030 hours, I crept past the grey bulk of HMS *Dunbarton Castle* to the accompaniment of a long blast on their whistle. Sixty-four days (forty-five of them without a mast) and over seven thousand miles had passed since we set sail from Sydney, Australia. *Joseph Young* had done me proud.

PART FOUR

Falkland Islands to Newport

A barrage of emotions overwhelmed me as I docked at East Cove. The relief I felt at simply having survived, the knowledge that the misery and frustration of the last month and a half was over, made everything that was happening to me now seem like a dream. There was no time, however, to wallow in quiet satisfaction or to dwell on what might have been. A small crowd of well-wishers was on hand to welcome me in and their presence required that I put aside such thoughts for the moment. Stepping ashore, standing upright, and acting as one of the human race again after so long alone took my full concentration. The Commanding Officer of the Falklands, Rear Admiral Chris Leyland, gave me an official greeting and put me in the charge of a liaison officer. I shook hands with everybody at the dock and thanked them for coming to see me in, and then found myself giving the local newspaper a short interview. HMS *Dunbarton Castle* was just coming alongside at the other side of the dock, so I walked shakily over to thank the captain profusely for his assistance. Dismissing it as a welcome diversion, he led me to his cabin, where I was left alone to clean up in preparation for a wardroom lunch with the ship's officers. Stripping off the layers of oilskins, sweaters, and thermal underwear, I stepped cautiously into the shower and turned on the water. Grinning from ear to ear, I revelled in the unending stream of hot, fresh, water. I knew, as I scrubbed away the accumulated grime and salt of the previous weeks that nothing could possibly have felt better. Eventually, with some reluctance, I shut off the water and faced the luxury of a dry towel and a set of clean clothes. I quickly bagged my dirty gear, surprised at how awful it smelt and found my way down to the wardroom where I was soon seated at a table resplendent with linen and silverware. Talk about culture shock!

I was disappointed to learn over lunch that my new mast would not arrive for another week. John Sandford, a close friend and key supporter from home, and Evert Bastet, whose company had put together the new mast, were coming down to help with the repairs to *Joseph Young* and were not due to fly in until tomorrow morning. Still, these were only minor delays and did nothing to dampen my enthusiasm for good food and real conversation.

After a long lunch, I was escorted down the wharf to another vessel, the M.V. *Stena Seaspread*, on charter to the Royal Navy, where I was allotted a cabin for the duration of my stay and introduced to key personnel in the military hierarchy. It was already obvious to me in the few hours that I had been ashore that co-operation was the name of the game as far as the British military on the Falklands was concerned. The remainder of the afternoon I spent ferrying two months' worth of dirty laundry from *Joseph Young* to my cabin aboard ship. By suppertime most of it had been washed and dried, and after another excellent meal I headed straight to bed. Crisp, clean sheets, soft pillows, a real mattress, and electric heat—I was soon lulled into a deep sleep.

I woke twelve hours later, much refreshed, and hurried through a shower and breakfast so that I could try to phone home to Vicki. Unfortunately, my efforts to phone Canada that day—and the following three days—were unsuccessful. International calls had to be made from the airport where a satellite link put one through to England. The operator then tried for a connection to Montreal, and the Canadian operator routed it from there to Halifax. It seemed that whenever I tried, one of the circuits was busy. A Land Rover and driver had been arranged to take me to the RAF airfield, where I could make my phone call and where I was to meet various air force personnel who would be handling arrangements for transporting the mast. They too, were more than helpful, and by the morning's end we had everything planned. John and Evert were due in shortly, so we adjourned to the mess hall for lunch.

No sooner had I sat down with a tray of food, than in came John. Jumping to my feet, I called across the room to him, and he turned and came running over to grip my hand. John introduced me to Evert, and over lunch they brought me up to date on affairs back in Nova Scotia. It had been nearly seven months since we had last seen each other, and there was a lot of catching up to do. The amount of support drummed up by the Dartmouth Yacht Club was overwhelming; it was their efforts that were making it possible for me to look forward to finishing the race.

Back at East Cove that afternoon, we confronted the shambles that was *Joseph Young*. We had six days before the new mast arrived, but clearly they would be six busy days; there was lots of work to be done. For the rest of that day, however, we simply planned and talked. We were all extremely tired, and we resolved to get a good night's sleep and start work refreshed in the morning.

Morning came and John, Evert, and I set to work on *Joseph Young*. A crate of spare parts had been sent on ahead of the mast, giving us the materials we needed to finish most of the preliminary repairs. Over the course of the next few days, the jury-rig was disassembled, and new chainplates, lifelines, bow pulpit, and mast step installed. The hole in the deck was fibreglassed properly, the generator overhauled, the batteries topped up, and the inside of the boat given a thorough clean. Working hard from breakfast until supper, the evenings more often than not spent partying with the military — it was an exhausting schedule.

On Monday, March 30, Evert and I went in to Port Stanley with the liaison officer. It was about a fifty-mile drive across a dirt track from East Cove and this was the only visit I made to the capital. Along the way we passed numerous roped-off areas — minefields left after the 1982 conflict. Stanley itself was a neat collection of mostly wooden houses, a few shops, a hospital, and the post office. In the harbour, the hulks of a dozen old sailing ships lay in various stages of rot, relics of the days when Port Stanley was the refuge of ships seeking shelter after losing their battle with Cape Horn. I thought with a quiet prayer of thanksgiving how close *Joseph Young* had come to joining their ranks.

Back at East Cove we stopped at the dock just long enough to pick up John before driving the three miles out to the airfield. The mast was due to arrive later that afternoon, and we wanted to be there when it did.

The Hercules transport aircraft carrying my mast was already rolled up at the off-loading bay when we arrived. A check of the cargo manifest showed that everything was on board, and we wasted no time in loading it all onto the waiting flatbed truck. It was hard for me to believe that my support committee back home had pulled it off; here I was on one of the most isolated islands in the world, taking receipt of a new rig for my yacht. It was an unprecedented feat of logistics.

Taking it nice and slowly, we covered the distance back to the dock area in half an hour. We had been given space in a warehouse in which to assemble the mast, and carrying the whole shipment inside, we began by uncrating the spars and removing the packing material. Now the real work could begin.

The mast had been shipped in two sections that had to be riveted and welded together. Spreaders, lights, fittings, mast-head instruments, and antennas all had to be installed. Standing and running rigging had to be cut to size and attached, wiring run, and sailtrack put in place. For the next three days we worked from eight in the morning right through until three or four the following morning. By noon on Thursday the mast was ready to be stepped. Unfortunately, however, the weather was not co-operating; winds of 35 to 40 knots were gusting across the harbour. As anxious as I was to get going, prudence played a winning hand, and we decided to wait until the next day, hoping that the wind would drop off. The plan was to lay the mast on the deck of *Joseph Young*, slide her over alongside a neighbouring cargo vessel, and use their deck crane to lift the spar into place. A small army of volunteers was lined up and everything was ready to go. All we needed was a little help from Mother Nature.

At breakfast the next day I looked glumly out at the weather. The anemometer on the ship's bridge was now registering winds of over 50 knots! A decision had to be reached. John and Evert were scheduled to fly out the following afternoon, and I needed Evert's expertise to tune the mast under sail. Throwing caution to the wind — literally — we agreed to go ahead as planned and step the mast. Rounding up our volunteer crew, we marched off to the warehouse, and, hefting the sixty-five-foot rig onto our massed shoulders we staggered the thousand yards or so down to the deck of *Joseph Young*. A short time later we were securely tied alongside the mother ship and on view; a sizeable crowd—which included Admiral Leyland—had gathered to watch and perhaps to help. Swallowing my fear of disaster, I gave the signal. Willing hands began to hoist away. Unbelievably, it all went without a hitch, and in what seemed like no time at all, *Joseph Young* looked like a proper yacht once again.

Back at our own wharf, we spent the rest of the day tightening up the shrouds and stays, rigging the halyards and sheets, setting up the boom, and putting on the new mainsail. Tomorrow we'd go sailing!

Saturday, April 4, dawned fine and clear. The wind was a perfect 15 to 20 knots, ideal for sea trials. Breakfast out of the way, the three of us hustled aboard *Joseph Young*, raised sail, and slipped the lines. Once clear of the wharf, she heeled over in the freshening breeze, spreading her new wings to the wind. At the tiller, a grin spread across my face as I felt my boat respond. This was how sailing was supposed to be.

For the next two hours we tacked back and forth across the

harbour as Evert worked on the rigging. Once he was satisfied, I turned the bow towards home. After two long months, *Joseph Young* was once again whole.

Back ashore, Evert packed a few last-minute things before John and I escorted him out to the airfield. John had decided to stay on in the Falklands until next week's flight, not wanting to leave until he had seen me safely on my way. When we had said good-bye to Evert, I walked over to the phones to try one last call home. After several attempts I was finally able to get through. Vicki had phoned me several times over the last ten days, but this parting conversation was the hardest yet. My leaving the safety of land for the open sea once more was a difficult step for both of us. Hanging up the phone, I was comforted by the thought that we should be together again in only six weeks' time.

That evening John and I stowed away the last of the stores, topped the water and fuel tanks, and shared a final drink. We discussed the upcoming voyage, and my chances of making it back to Newport in time for the prize-giving. For me, this remained my personal, crucial, goal. On the face of it, attaining that goal looked like a good possibility. With about 7,000 miles to go, I would need to average 125 miles per day, or 5.2 knots. That sort of speed was certainly within *Joseph Young*'s capability, but did not allow any margin for breakdowns or calm weather. After struggling so hard for so long, it would be devastating to be beaten on the final lap.

The rest of the fleet was due to depart Rio a week from today. Obviously, I had hoped to join them for this last leg, but the delay in getting the mast to the Falklands had put paid to that idea. Still, I should be able to maintain radio contact with them for most of the trip, which would be a real morale booster.

After a leisurely breakfast, I spent the following morning doing a final laundry and packing away clothes aboard the boat. The truth of the matter was that I felt quite nervous about setting off again, and I welcomed any small delay. After thirteen nights in the Falklands I had become accustomed to the comforts of civilization and the company of others. By lunchtime, however, there were no more plausible reasons for me to put off my departure, so, after a quick meal, John and I walked down to the wharf for the last time. A crowd of my new-found friends had come out to wish me well. I would not soon forget the way in which they had made me feel welcome here, helping me out in a time of real need. After handshakes all round, the lines were let go, and *Joseph Young* moved gently off the dock. We proceeded under tow down the harbour while sail was hoisted. All too quickly, the time came for me to cut my last ties with the land, and, bidding me a final farewell, John cast off the tow and hopped off into the escorting power boat. When they turned back, I watched until the small boat had disappeared from view. Putting aside my anxiety, I steered *Joseph Young* down the channel towards the open sea. It was three o'clock on the afternoon of April 5. The final leg of a very long voyage had begun.

With the wind from the south-west at Force 4, *Joseph Young* reached quickly eastwards along the coast of the Falklands. The sky was almost clear, the sea quite smooth, and the air crisp and cool. I could not have asked for better weather to see me away from the land. I planned to stay up through the night, as large numbers of trawlers were working the waters around the islands. By morning we should be heading north towards Rio, having rounded the eastern tip of the Falklands.

After an hour or two, I began to relax a bit about being back at sea again. I had almost forgotten what it was like to sail with a full rig and mast. It seemed I was forever trimming the sails and tweaking one of the numerous control lines, trying to get everything in proper racing trim. The motion of the boat with all that weight aloft was unbelievably smooth, and under full sail *Joseph Young* was once again slicing through the water like the true thoroughbred that she was. I couldn't have been happier.

Shortly after sunset the wind started to increase, and, unused as yet to the new rigging arrangement, I clumsily took a couple of reefs in the mainsail. By 2300 the headsail had to be changed for something a little smaller, as the south-westerly breeze was now almost up to gale force. I was loving every minute of it! The first night passed quickly, and in the early hours of dawn the wind shifted abruptly to the north-west and dropped to a light Force 3. Hoisting more sail to keep the speed up, I allowed *Joseph Young* to come on to a more northerly heading before dropping below for breakfast. I soon had a good feed of fresh eggs and bacon sizzling in the pan, accompanied by real bread and honest butter—I felt I was truly living in the lap of luxury.

Throughout that morning I busied myself on deck, rerigging some of the lines a little more to my satisfaction. A grey, overcast sky and a cold, intermittent drizzle served to remind me that I was still a good week away from the blue skies and hot sunshine of the tropics.

After a lunch of bread and cheese washed down with a mug of tea, I made up the settee berth for a much-needed sleep. In the Falklands, I had been given a new down-filled sleeping bag. The old, smelly, mildew-blackened one I had ceremoniously disposed of before leaving, and now I really looked forward to my warm, dry, odour-free cocoon. It was so warm, in fact, that I was able to sleep without my clothes on, despite the still low temperatures. Snuggled down into the folds of olive-green, lulled by the happy sound of water rushing by the hull, I drifted off to sleep.

The next three days passed quickly, both myself and the weather having established a definite pattern. During the days, the sailing was just great, moderate winds from the north-west being the norm. Although the wind and sea were still cold, it was never too rough, and progress was good. At night, however, the wind would die away to nearly nothing, leaving *Joseph Young* to creep northward under a canopy of beautifully bright stars. I soon learned to regulate myself accordingly, snatching sleep during the days, and spending the nights coaxing what speed I could from the boat. Sailing quietly along in the darkness I felt more relaxed than I had done in months. Gone was the constant, nagging fear of violent weather and the prospect of Cape Horn. Behind me lay two weeks of frantic preparation to ready *Joseph Young* for sea. Now, I looked forward with confidence to each sunrise, every day bringing me closer to home. It was a regimen that I thoroughly enjoyed.

On the evening of April 9 the wind began to increase until it was blowing a full gale. For the next fifty hours I had my hands full as the seas built to dangerous proportions, keeping me at the tiller for long spells and forcing continual reductions in the amount of sail I was carrying. Much to my annoyance, I found that I was cowed by the heavy weather, very much afraid that the new mast might also be lost. As we punched and rolled our way through wave after wave I gazed skeptically aloft, wondering at the engineering that allowed such a tall mast to be supported by this spiderweb of wires and bolts. I shuddered at every little creak and groan that reverberated through the hull.

In my mind's eye, each new noise was the forerunner of disaster. I realized sadly that my confidence in the new rig was as yet sorely lacking.

Finally, just before midnight on April 11, the cold front that had brought such miserable weather passed, bowing out in a spectacular display of lightning and heavy rain. For the next three hours *Joseph Young* lay virtually becalmed in a cold drizzle until the wind finally settled down to a moderate south-west breeze. I wasted no time in hoisting full sail, and we were soon moving comfortably along on course for Rio. I was pleased, and more than a little surprised, that we had come through this latest blow unscathed. Perhaps my fears were exaggerated. Perhaps, I thought, as I looked at the mileage covered since I had left the Falklands, I was playing too timid a hand. I resolved to push harder in the weeks to come. I was going to make it to Newport before the end of May.

As dawn broke on April 12, the sky cleared rapidly until there was not a cloud to be seen. The temperature climbed with the sun, reaching an amazing 19°C by the afternoon. Peeling off layers of cold-weather clothing I revelled in the heat, noting in the log book my first sighting of flying fish since before Cape Town. This was what I had been dreaming of for so long!

That evening, coffee in hand, I sat by the radio trying to establish contact with the other competitors. I knew that the frequencies and schedules for the chat hour would have been altered for the last leg, so I didn't hold out much hope. I was just about to give up when I heard, faintly in the background, Ian Kiernan, the lone Australian in the race. Quickly, I put out a call and was overjoyed when he responded. After we had caught up on some of the news, Ian was able to put me in touch with a few of the others. At long last I felt as if I was truly back in the race.

As I talked to the other competitors, a picture of the stopover in Rio gradually unfolded that left me with the realization that I had one more bridge to cross. I heard stories of lengthy delays and endless red tape at the hands of customs officials, poor services, currency problems, robberies, and the inevitable South American *mañana*, all of which led me to one simple conclusion. If I was forced to enter the port of Rio in order to comply with the rules of the race, I could expect to be there for no less than one week. To add to the problem, all the race officials were planning to leave before my arrival, which meant I would be left entirely on my own to deal with the locals. With a sinking heart, I knew that this "Brazilian Factor" would kill any chance I had of making Newport in time.

Later that night, I got on the radio again to place a call home and to transmit my concerns to the Race Committee. As it turned out, Race Chairman Robin Knox-Johnston, bless him, had foreseen my predicament and had an option ready to offer me. He would arrange for a boat to meet me outside the mouth of the harbour to witness my crossing of the finish line for the third leg and my subsequent re-start for the fourth. I would thus manage to avoid the necessity of formally entering the country and could be on my way again in a matter of hours. The light at the end of my tunnel began to glow a little brighter; without the slightest hesitation I agreed to this strategy. Frequencies and times for radio communications between myself and the Rio Committee boat were established, and an order was taken for a resupply of bottled water and fresh fruit. Things were definitely looking up.

The next four days brought perhaps the finest sailing of the voyage to date. Although a touch on the light side, the wind remained favourable in direction and *Joseph Young* gradually closed to within four hundred miles of Rio de Janeiro. The sky was always blue, the temperature in the low-to-mid-twenties, and pilot whales, porpoises, and flying fish abounded. Being at sea in these conditions was pure pleasure. But, of course, it was too good to last.

At 0200 on April 16 I awoke to the terrible sound of flogging sailcloth. Having fallen asleep dressed in shorts and safety harness, I was up on deck in a flash. The wind, which had been from the south-east when I turned in, had now shifted round to the north-north-east — the very direction in which I wanted to head. It had also increased substantially, making it wet going as we slogged to windward. In disgust, I noted in the log-book: *Rough sea. Hard going to windward. Normal procedure for* Joseph Young *to have headwinds of gale force within two days of a landfall. Need wind shift!*

This brief blow ended the following afternoon, leaving us wallowing helplessly in a calm. It seemed that making port was definitely not our forte. The temperature soared to an unbearable 30°C, sapping my strength and taxing my patience. Frequent salt-water showers provided some relief. An old coffee can with a line attached was used to draw water from over the side and dump it over my head. *Luxury* is a purely relative term.

The next morning, stage two of my well-polished land-approach technique came into play. The satellite navigator stopped working. Repaired by the Royal Navy as well as could be expected without the proper parts, it now gave up the ghost altogether. At this point, I was less than two hundred miles from the finish line and only about forty miles off the Brazilian coast. That was the bad news, but there was some good news; the wind finally returned just before supper. I opted to close with the coast and run eastward along the shore to Rio, so I set my course accordingly and turned in for a quick nap before it got dark. The presence of numerous merchant ships would preclude my getting any proper sleep again until after I had left Rio.

April 19, 1987
24 16S 44 22W

0300 hours: I sighted the light on Punta do Boi an hour ago, and am now tacking eastward along the coast. The visibility is perfect, fortunately, as the number of ships and fishing vessels passing me in the darkness is surprising. I haven't seen such traffic as this since my departure from Sydney.

The sunrise a few hours after this diary entry was simply spectacular. As the darkness gradually gave way to the early light of dawn, the towering mountains of the Brazilian coast slowly took form off my port side. From a black silhouette, they took on a shade of deep purple, finally showing off a covering of rich green vegetation as the sun climbed above the horizon. The scenery provided a welcome diversion for the rest of the day as *Joseph Young* and I slowly clawed our way closer to the finish line in the face of the light easterly breeze. Shortly after lunch, a pod of whales was sighted close in off the starboard bow. As a precaution I started the generator, hoping that the noise would alert them to my presence. For over an hour I watched as these huge mammals moved slowly inshore, graceful in spite of their bulk. If the feeble putt-putt of my nine-horsepower generator alarmed them at all, they certainly didn't let it show.

As the day wore on, I was becoming increasingly concerned about the rendezvous off Rio. I had been unable to make radio contact with the yacht club on any of the pre-arranged frequencies, and attempts to place a call through the marine radio station were hampered by my not speaking Portuguese. I could only hope that the Race Committee was keeping a close eye on my Argos positions and passing the information along to their representative in Rio.

When daylight came the following morning, *Joseph Young* was lying stopped in the water only fifteen miles from the finish line. The wind had died completely at 0200, leaving me tired and frustrated. I hadn't had a decent sleep now for two days, and I needed desperately to get in and out of Rio and clear of the land by nightfall. I knew I would have to have some rest by tonight, and I was afraid I might pass out before we were offshore once again. Ready to try anything, I began to whistle for the wind, any wind, to see me safely through.

By eight o'clock the sun had been up for a few hours. Occasional light puffs of wind were stirring the water around me. With a lot of coaxing, *Joseph Young* began to ghost forward in short spurts, giving me hope, if not much speed. After three hours of this agony we had finally worked our way past the last of the islands that lay scattered between us and the finish. Repeated calls on the VHF radio to the Committee boat had so far brought no response, but suddenly I heard them calling me. With a feeling of immense relief I replied, giving them my position, and within half an hour they hove into sight, racing in my direction. Once they were within hailing distance, we exchanged greetings, and they assured me that the wind was bound to fill in soon. Somewhat skeptical, I settled down to wait some more, and half-hour later they were proven right; a light southerly breeze arrived at last. All smiles now, I trimmed the sails and set off to cover the remaining two miles. At twenty-eight minutes past noon on April 20, *Joseph Young* nudged her bow across the finish line marking the end of the third leg. Three months and a little over nine thousand miles had passed since we had set out from Sydney, Australia. This stage of the race had not been an easy one for either my boat or myself.

I wasted no time in dropping the sails and accepting a tow from the committee boat. The plan was to proceed to anchor off Copacabana Beach, where it would be easier to transfer the requested supply of bottled water and fruit across to *Joseph Young*. In no time at all we were rafted alongside each other, swinging lazily to a single anchor dropped by the Committee boat. A bottle of champagne was popped by the local BOC representative, officially welcoming me to Brazil. For an hour, we sat around in the sweltering heat, sipping on the bubbly while I answered questions on the events of the past few months. Once the magnum was empty, willing hands passed over cases of bottled water and bags of fresh fruit, coffee, and ice. A bundle of mail from home and a copy of the race instructions for the final portion of the trip were stowed below for later reading. Then, while volunteers emptied the water into the tanks aboard *Joseph Young*, I slipped aboard the Committee boat for a cold, fresh-water shower. By three o'clock we were ready to depart. Having been at sea only fifteen days since leaving the Falklands, I didn't feel any great urge to go ashore. Admittedly, when I had set out from Sydney, the idea of a month's holiday in Rio had held a certain appeal, but with the rest of the competitors now hundreds of miles ahead of me on the road home, the attraction was gone. The only thing on my mind was to get underway—to push on for Newport. There were only forty days still remaining before the prize-giving ceremonies, and 5,100 miles still to sail.

Casting off the lines holding *Joseph Young* alongside the Committee boat, I drifted astern to take up the tow line. As soon as the anchor was aweigh, we proceeded out to the start-line area. Twenty minutes later I dropped the tow and hoisted the main and Genoa, an exhausting job in the heat of mid-afternoon. The light wind that still persisted was just sufficient to fill the sails, and, heeling gently, we began to gather way. At 1529 local time, three hours after finishing leg three, *Joseph Young* and I crossed the start line to begin the fourth and final portion of the trip. A blast on the whistle and a wave of hands from the Committee boat sent us on our way. For the last time, I pointed the bow towards the open sea, and watched as the land receded into our wake.

As the evening twilight gradually faded into darkness, the glow of Rio's lights was still visible on the northern horizon. Towering black clouds that had formed over the mountains late in the afternoon seemed to have had no effect on the winds farther offshore, and *Joseph Young* continued to slip along in the faint breeze. Several westbound ships had been sighted earlier on, but for now the ocean belonged only to us. My eyes heavy with fatigue, the electric steering following a course which would take us safely away from land, I decided to take a short nap in the cockpit. Setting the alarm to wake me in an hour, I padded the deck with the sleeping bag dragged from below and lay down to sleep.

I awoke with a start, the morning sun warm upon my face. In panic I sat up, expecting to find us about to run ashore, or to be smashed into oblivion by an unseeing ship. Frantically I gazed around the horizon. Nothing. No land; no ships. Much relieved, I looked at the time and cursed myself for an idiot. I had been asleep for a good ten hours! Guiltily I bundled up the sleeping bag and tossed it down the hatch. After another quick check on the course and the sails, I climbed below to put on some coffee. Luck alone had kept me safe through the night. This had been a mistake that could have cost me, as it had others, dearly. It was a sobering thought.

For the rest of the day the wind remained light, giving me a chance to catch up on some jobs on board. The #3 jib had been damaged several days previously and needed a few hours with a needle and thread to put it back in shape. Stores were re-stowed, and after I had read through the race instructions, the single-sideband radio had to be programmed with new frequencies. With the satellite navigator now not working at all, more time also had to set aside for navigation.

In that heat, the huge sack of fresh fruit that I had been given in Rio tasted wonderful, although I never did find out exactly what it was I was eating. It looked exactly like an orange except with a green skin; it was tart and refreshing, and I hoped that consuming four or five a day wouldn't have an adverse effect on my system. One of the other surprises from Rio had been the block of ice put aboard *Joseph Young*. I hadn't bothered with ice before, reasoning that it wouldn't last long enough to be worthwhile. Now I found that being able to have a really cold cup of water was a treat.

That evening the wind strengthened quickly as the sun went down, rising to near gale force from the east. Lightning flickered almost continuously around the horizon, and I quickly reduced sail in anticipation of a major blow. All night I tacked to windward, wishing that the wind would shift to a more favourable direction. Until we had cleared the south-eastern tip of Brazil we couldn't bear off and take advantage of this gale. Catnapping whenever possible, I passed a slow and uncomfortable night.

The next day was not much better, weatherwise; the easterly wind continued to make for hard going. Looking over the charts for the area between here and the equator I realized that I faced a tactical decision. Traditionally, there were two routes for sailing ships to take when bound from the Brazilian seaboard to North Atlantic ports. The first option was to stay close inshore all the way up the coast, thus avoiding the south-flowing current farther offshore. Precise navigation and vigilance were needed to follow the coastline and to avoid the numerous fishing and commercial vessels on this route. Oilfields being developed close along the shore posed an additional hazard. The second option was to get farther offshore as soon as possible, taking advantage of the stronger south-east trade winds to sail quickly north. This course avoided the inherent dangers of the inshore route.

Weighing the pros and cons of my situation, I didn't take too long to decide on the offshore option. With the satellite navigator out of operation, I would be relying on navigation by the sun and stars only. If the sky clouded over, it meant I would have no way of fixing *Joseph Young*'s position, not a pleasant prospect if I were threading my way up the shore. Fatigue, too, played its part in the decision. I hadn't had regular sleep for some time now, and oversleeping as I had the other night could prove fatal on the inshore route. Remembering the long days of steady trade winds and blue skies on the outward voyage, when I had passed only fifty to a hundred miles of this very coast, was the clincher.

Unfortunately my dreams of a fast, pleasant sail north to the equator were never realized. The next six days turned into a nightmare of unsettled weather, exhausting sailing, and complete frustration. During the days, the wind blew from the north or north-east, varying continuously in strength from very light to gale force. It never seemed to settle down for more than an hour or two before I found myself frantically changing sails again, hauling down over-pressed canvas on the foredeck as *Joseph Young* keeled over to a ferocious gale, or hoisting larger and lighter sails in an effort to keep her moving in a dying breeze. In the intense heat and humidity, every mile had to be fought for. If the days were bad, the nights were worse.

Almost without fail, the wind would die completely with the setting sun, as if gathering its strength for an attack under cover of darkness. With the fading of daylight, lightning would become visible, dancing around on the horizon like the flashes of distant gunfire. Resigned, I would move to reduce sail again, knowing what to expect. *Joseph Young* and I, becalmed, could only drift and wait, though far from patiently. Sometimes I could hear the wind coming before it struck; sometimes it would be preceded by a torrential rain shower. From which direction it blew, however, was always a guess. When it hit, *Joseph Young* would take off as I hastily trimmed the sails, tacked, or gybed, trying to head in a favourable direction. In the pitch dark, with only the dim red glow of the compass for a reference, it was easy to become disoriented. These squalls were mostly of short duration, and within an hour we would be left to drift again, awaiting the next onslaught. I was tired, wet, and exasperated; my nerves were stretched taut, and daylight seemed a long time coming. Progress, not surprisingly, was dismal.

After six days of this misery, the weather changed, though hardly for the better. On the evening of April 28 the wind died in the evening as usual, but instead of the normal succession of squalls, there was absolutely nothing. All night I sat in the cockpit, the boat rolling gently in the low swell, sails slatting, and I waited and wondered. Stars were visible through the broken cloud above. It would have been a beautiful night if I hadn't been concerned about making miles. When dawn came, it brought very little change. Occasional zephyrs stirred the sails, moving us slowly forward, but real wind was nowhere to be found. The sun beat down, driving the temperature up to 32°C in the shade. What little patience I had left was evaporating rapidly.

For the next three days we crept north in the unrelentingly light winds, my morale, and my hopes of reaching Newport on time, sinking to a new low. By noon on May 1 I had covered less than one-quarter of the last leg of the race. At this rate I simply was not going to make it. My average speed since leaving Rio was a mere 4.5 knots. I needed 5.3 knots to finish on time. In search of better wind, I decided to close with the coast in the vicinity of Recife. Something had to change.

On May 2 I woke from a short nap at three-thirty in the morning and set about preparing breakfast. My diet had become a little monotonous over the last couple of weeks. Relying almost exclusively on army field rations obtained in the Falklands, I had become a "can-opener cook" in the truest sense of the word. Breakfast invariably, consisted of beans (canned) and sausages (canned), a concoction that required vast quantities of tea to wash it down. For lunch and/or supper, I could choose from delicacies such as meat and vegetables (canned), steak and kidney pudding (canned), and apple suet pudding (canned). Rumour in the Falklands had it that all of these dishes should be enjoyed with a side order of your favourite laxative, as they were all purported to be laced with a substance designed to prevent embarrassing evidence of fear in combat.

After tidying up the breakfast dishes, I settled into the cockpit to keep a lookout. According to my most recent position, I should sight land shortly after sunrise. At 0500 hours, almost on schedule, the coastline of Brazil hove into sight over the horizon. Sailing in to a distance of a few miles off the shore, I began tacking northwards into the wind. The presence of numerous small, open, fishing boats worried me a little, as I remembered all the stories I had been told about piracy on this coast. They seemed not the slightest bit interested in me, however, and as the morning wore on I began to feel a little more relaxed.

At 1400 hours I noted in the log-book: *Wind shifted to easterly at Force 4. Favourable wind? Must be a mistake.* This time, though, my cynicism was unfounded, and for the rest of the day, and throughout the following night, the wind held from the east. *Joseph Young* sliced through the water on a reach, giving me great sailing for the first time in what seemed weeks.

Early afternoon the following day found me gliding slowly past the skyline of Recife, one of Brazil's larger port cities. The amount of pollution and refuse in the water was shocking, and I was glad when the wind picked up again, speeding me on my way north, clear of such unpleasant signs of civilization. I was hoping to leave the coastline and the shipping lanes behind me by midnight so that I could catch a little sleep. Fortunately, all went well, and by two in the morning I felt safe enough to fall asleep in the cockpit for four hours. I wouldn't, I hoped, see land again until Newport.

May 4 marked a turning-point in my luck. The day started well with a heavy, prolonged downpour of warm rain. Shucking my clothes, I grabbed the shampoo and soap, and dashed on deck to enjoy a morning shower. It made a refreshing change from my usual salt-water bath. Later on, at 1230, *Joseph Young* crossed her outward track from the voyage between Newport and Cape Town. It seemed strange to think of us being in exactly this same spot some seven and a half months ago, southbound and virtually untested. A lot had happened to both of us in the days and weeks since. I had closed the circle and now I felt that the end of my personal pilgrimage was rapidly approaching. *Joseph Young* and I had become very used to this world of wind and water. I wondered what it would be like not to have the next obstacle, the next ocean, and the next port to look ahead to.

Later that same afternoon the trade winds, which had been so elusive, came to stay, blowing a solid Force 5 from the south-east. By the following noon, *Joseph Young* had logged a day's run of two hundred miles at an average speed of 8.3 knots. This was more like it! My spirits, so easily changed by my immediate physical circumstances, rose quickly. Perhaps I did still have a chance of arriving in Newport before the end of May. Tempering this were reports I had received from the boats far to the north, now within six hundred or seven hundred miles of the finish. Plagued by light winds and strong currents, some of them had come to a virtual standstill. Mark Schrader even reported being set backwards by the current during one twenty-four-hour period. I said a silent prayer for improved conditions in the Gulf Stream before my arrival there. The thought of entering Newport one or two days after the prize-giving ceremonies did not bear thinking about.

The next day, May 6, at 1430 hours, I crossed the equator and left the South Atlantic Ocean behind. Being in the northern hemisphere again felt like being in home waters. For an hour and a half, a large number of dolphins swam alongside the boat, weaving in and out of the bow wave, so close that their breathing was clearly audible. As always, they held me spellbound with their graceful antics. When they finally disappeared for good, I felt a sense of loss; I wanted to shout out to them to stay a while longer.

Although the south-east trades stayed with me, the weather became increasingly squally as the afternoon waned. Remembering the agony of the doldrums on the outward trip, I anxiously watched for a change in the weather, hoping feverishly that I would be spared a repeat performance. Since early that morning a noticeable swell had been rolling in from the north-east. Although it made the sailing distinctly uncomfortable, it gave me reason to hope that the north-east trades were not too far away, and were blowing strong and steady. With the weather facsimile recorder now defunct, I had no way of knowing what lay ahead. It had to be simply a matter of "wait-and-see."

For the last two weeks, ever since leaving Rio really, the radio reception, hampered by the frequent lightning and squalls off the Brazilian coast, had been quite poor. Tonight, however, I was determined that I would get a call through to Vicki, and I stayed up until the early hours of morning to place it. The American stations in Miami and Oceangate were very efficient, as always, and once they had tuned in to my signal they were able to make an almost perfect connection to home. Talking to Vicki gave me renewed hope, and kindled a flood of emotions and excitement at the prospect of our reunion after so long apart. A large group of family and friends were planning a mass excursion to Newport to welcome me in. There were obviously a lot of people counting on me; all the more reason to push myself harder for the remaining few weeks. When we eventually broke the connection, it took me several hours to wind down enough to feel like sleeping. I replayed our conversation over and over in my mind until the sun was almost above the horizon before I finally crawled into the sleeping bag.

Early in the evening of May 7 the south-east trade winds suddenly collapsed, giving way to squally weather. Heavy showers of rain accompanied the squalls, and virtual calms in between left me with a terrible fear that I was now in the clutches of the dreaded doldrums. After two hours of this I was beside myself with frustration, certain that this was going to be the straw to break the back of my dreams, when suddenly a light breeze filled in from the north-east. Scarcely daring to breathe, from some foolish notion that I might actually frighten the wind away, I moved slowly and carefully around the deck, trimming the sails for maximum effect. Until long after dark I stayed at the tiller, squeezing as many miles as possible from the unsteady wind. By midnight the wind had strengthened considerably, so, leaving the self-steering in charge, I disappeared below for a nap.

Next morning on the chat hour I heard from Mark that six of the Class-One boats had arrived in Newport the previous day. With just under three thousand miles still to go, that certainly gave me food for thought. As it turned out, the north-east trade winds had indeed come to stay, and for the next five days *Joseph*

Young romped along in almost ideal conditions, eating up the distance.

At 0200 hours on May 12, I settled myself back into the settee berth after a brief spell on deck shaking out a reef in the mainsail. Just as I was about asleep, I was jerked awake again by soft thudding noises, followed by a brief "pitter-patter" from up on deck. Swinging quickly out of the bunk, I grabbed the flashlight and went to investigate. From the safety of the cockpit I shone the light around the boat. *Joseph Young* had been boarded by a school of flying fish! Winging their way clear of the water, they had flown head-first into the mast and sails, bouncing off to land on the deck. Relieved that that was all it was, I returned below for another attempt at sleep. In the morning I picked up a good four dozen of the small fish and dropped them back into the sea. Not more than four or five inches long, they seemed to be all eyes and fins, rather unappealing as breakfast, even when compared to yet more sausages and beans.

A little later on in the day I heard via the radio that the last of the other competitors had arrived in Newport that morning. I felt a bit depressed and very, very alone when I thought of the miles still remaining between me and the final finish line.

Eventually the inevitable happened; we sailed out from under the influence of the trade winds and into that area known as the Horse Latitudes. For three long days I changed headsails, reefed and unreefed, tacked, gybed, hoisted and doused spinnakers, baked in the hot sun, got soaked by rain and drizzle, all the while cursing and struggling to keep the boat moving northward. The speed dropped dramatically; in one twenty-four-hour period we covered a pathetic seventy-five miles! The pressure of the May 30 deadline hanging over me was taking its toll, wearing my patience thin and causing me to explode in anger at the slightest provocation.

Watching the sunrise on the morning of May 16 I was just about at the end of my tether. Another miserable night of calms and drizzle had passed with me at the tiller. What few puffs of wind there had been were merely teasers, lasting for a few minutes at best. With the sun, though, came a gentle breeze from the north-east, just enough to allow the auto-pilot to maintain the course while I slipped below to make some coffee. Back on deck a short while later, I watched with interest as the faint silhouette of a ship on the horizon drew nearer. Eventually, as it passed no more than half a mile astern of *Joseph Young*, I could see that she was a small Japanese fishing trawler. Despite repeated attempts to contact her on the radio, I received no reply, and could only watch as she slowly chugged her way east until lost from view.

After lunch the wind freshened considerably, bringing with it a rapid rise in my morale. Inspired, I decided that a little cleaning was in order, and I spent the next five hours scrubbing the interior of the boat and oiling some of the teak trim. This, as I noted in the log-book, brought about an unbelievable transformation.

On the starboard tack, *Joseph Young* was moving along nicely in the flat sea, slicing through great swathes of sargasso weed floating on the surface. It was a beautiful day, and I was more than content just to sit on deck and let the self-steering do the work. When noon came, I went below to fetch the sextant for a sight of the sun. It was while I was peering southwards through the instrument's telescope that I spotted the thin outline of a mast in the distance. As soon as I had finished the noon sight, I dug out the binoculars for a better look. Sure enough, it was another sailboat. Turning on the VHF radio, I was surprised to hear a voice calling "the northbound sloop just ahead of me." Replying, I identified myself, and found that I was talking to the French yacht *Astragale*, bound from Martinique to the Azores. Talking to Loic Lepage, who was also single-handing, I agreed to pass on a message to his wife, as he did not have a radio for long-distance communication. This brief contact with another yacht was a real pleasure. Since the last of the other BOC competitors had arrived in port almost a week ago, I had missed the conversations about wind, weather, and sailing. After talking for a good ten minutes, Loic and I wished each other a safe voyage and signed off the air. Before long his mast was lost to view.

A short time later the electronic log, or speedometer, stopped working, showing a reading of 0 knots while *Joseph Young* was still moving along nicely. With the amount of sargasso weed that we had been sailing through, this came as no real surprise. The log impeller had obviously become fouled. It was essential that I clear it, not a difficult job but one that always made me a little nervous. Lifting the floorboards to expose the impeller unit, I removed the safety clip that prevented the unit from accidentally coming free of its own accord. Holding the dummy plug in my left hand, I grasped the handle of the impeller plug in my right hand, and gave it a half twist to unlock it from the fitting that held it in the hull. Now, the trick here was to be quick. Taking a deep breath, I pulled the impeller unit straight up, opening a two-inch hole in the bottom of the boat. A fountain of sea water poured into the cabin during the few seconds it took me to ram the dummy plug into the hole. My over-active imagination always played a scenario where neither the dummy plug nor the impeller would go back into the through-hull fitting. In reality, this was a simple little chore. Looking at the impeller, I could see that what I had suspected was exactly what had happened; a strand of weed had become ensnared in the blades, preventing them from turning. With the blades cleaned, it was merely a matter of repeating the process, replacing the impeller unit in the hole. Satisfied, the excitement over, I returned to the cockpit.

That evening the wind died. Again. It was almost too much to bear. There were eleven hundred miles still to go, and only ten days left in which to go them. With good wind I could be home in six days. There was also the possibility that *Joseph Young* and I could be drifting around out here, becalmed, for many more days. I knew, deep down, that there was absolutely nothing that I could do, but it was an awful lot to have to swallow.

At this point I was only about four hundred miles from Bermuda. I felt somehow that if I could just get past this last obstacle, the rest would take care of itself. For the next two days I fretted and struggled, sleeping little as I tried every trick in the book to keep *Joseph Young* moving in the fickle wind. In the early hours of the morning of May 22 I was finally rewarded with a good strong north-easter. Almost too strong, in fact. Thrashing our way to windward, we covered a respectable 180 miles in the next twenty-four hours, passing to the east of Bermuda during the hours of darkness. Following this milestone I turned in for some much-needed rest, but I hadn't been asleep for more than two hours when the sound of engines, growing louder, dragged me back into the real world. Listening, I realized with relief that what I was hearing was the sound of a low-flying aircraft, not an approaching ship. Gradually the noise faded into the distance, leaving me secure in the warmth of my bunk.

Once again that afternoon the wind began to fail, and by evening there was not even enough of a breeze to fill the lightest spinnaker on board. Reluctantly, I took down the large sail and hoisted in its place the #1 Genoa. Another long night was spent at the helm, our speed never rising above 1.5 knots. I began to suspect that this pattern of frustration, hopes raised and then dashed by the inconsistency of the wind, was going to last right up until the finish.

On cue, sunrise the next morning brought an increasing breeze. By 0800 hours, *Joseph Young* was once more clipping along to a moderate south-wester. It was May 24, and we had only five hundred miles to go. At this point, I began to feel a new confidence growing within me. Nothing short of absolute calm lasting for several days could stop us from reaching Newport in time. Apart from the wind, or lack of wind, the only other factor of real concern at this point was the navigation as I approached land. With the sextant providing my only means of obtaining the boat's position, I desperately needed clear skies for the last few hundred miles. If the sun and stars were obscured by cloud or fog, it would be impossible for me to determine where I was. The only safe option as I closed with the coast under these circumstances would be to wait offshore until an accurate position could be taken. More than ever, I kept my fingers crossed, hoping for a little luck to come my way.

For a week now I had been in direct contact with Goat Island Marina in Newport via single-sideband radio. Talking to Peter

Dunning, one of the race organizers, on a daily basis was fuelling my excitement about finishing the race to a fever pitch. Sleeping, even relaxing, was becoming almost impossible for me. I imagined Vicki, my mother, my brother David, and my friends from Nova Scotia crowding around the radio ashore, listening for my position reports. Through Peter, they passed on words of encouragement, urging me to hurry on in. I wanted to be there so badly I could hardly stand it, and would have to spend a few minutes after each conversation calming myself down. It was hard for me to believe that a long-awaited reunion with Vicki and the completion of my four-year dream were really only days away.

At 0300 on May 26 I lay down in the bunk aboard *Joseph Young* for the last time in the race. Since late the previous evening I had been on deck, steadily reducing sail as a near gale piped up from the north-east. This strong wind was both good and bad; it meant that we were now making good speed, but we were doing so under complete cloud cover. Land was now only twenty-four hours away, and I needed some good positions to put my mind at ease. Though I was tired, sleep did not come easily.

Four hours later I was up again, roused by the alarm clock. In the short, steep sea, we were making hard going of it, throwing spray everywhere as we crashed through the waves. Dressing in my well-worn oilskins, I struggled reluctantly up into the cockpit for a check of the boat and weather. I was a little startled to see a large cargo ship no more than two miles ahead of us, crossing our track as she headed off to the west. I wondered if we had even been sighted amongst the whitecaps. From now on, a continuous lookout was obviously called for.

To my immense relief the barometer had risen slightly by noon, and as the afternoon wore on the wind began to ease and veer more to the east. Gradually the sky cleared until only a few clouds remained. Perhaps, after all, I still had a small store of luck in hand. As twilight drew near, I prepared more carefully than ever for a round of star sights. It was absolutely crucial that I obtain an accurate position, as, at the rate we were going, we should be passing Block Island shortly before sunrise, leaving little room for error.

As soon as the evening sun dropped below the horizon, I was on deck, sextant in hand. Half an hour later, after some quick work with pencil and paper, I was able to mark a definite position on the chart. Greatly reassured, I altered course slightly to take me two miles to the east of Block Island. The finish line off Newport lay a mere sixty-seven miles ahead!

By 0100, true to form, the wind had all but quit. It was the ultimate cruel joke. Although I had hoisted the light #1 Genoa in place of the #3, we were still barely moving. Fortunately, there was just enough wind for the auto-pilot to take care of the steering so I decided to put the time to good use. Down in the cabin, I put a full kettle of water on to boil and slipped a tape into the cassette player. With no need to conserve fresh water now, I had decided to have a good wash. I stripped and, shivering slightly in the crisp air, I enjoyed a shampoo, sponge bath, and a shave. I soon felt in much better spirits. Hell, I thought, with only forty miles to go, I would be ashore by nightfall even if I had to paddle! From the closet I retrieved the shirt and pants, carefully pressed and wrapped in plastic, that I had set aside for this occasion before I had left the Falklands. I hung them up, ready to put on, and, after tidying up the cabin I slipped back on deck to resume a watch.

As the first glimmer of dawn spread across the sky, fishing boats began appearing, motoring out for the morning's catch. I peered through a very light haze, searching for the outline of land. At 0800, just a little off schedule, Block Island showed itself off the port bow, identifiable by the flash of its lighthouse. Visibility, I estimated, was about two miles. A short time later the rising sun began burning off the haze, bringing with it a slight freshening of the breeze from the south-east. Working as fast as I could, I hoisted the spinnaker to take advantage of the wind, watching with satisfaction as the speed crept up over 7 knots. Things were happening quickly now. At 0900 hours I called Goat Island according to our pre-arranged schedule, passing along my estimated time of arrival for 1130 hours. I also spoke with Mark Schrader, motoring out to meet me aboard *Lone Star*.

No more than half an hour later, while I was down below on the radio arranging a rendezvous with Mark, I felt a change in the boat's motion. Dashing up on deck, I was dismayed to see that the wind had abandoned us, leaving me once again well and truly becalmed. In the distance, I could see the bridge spanning the harbour in Newport, ten miles away at most. This was becoming *really* frustrating.

Twenty minutes later my anxiety over the lack of wind was put to the back of my mind as *Lone Star* arrived on the scene. Mark and I shouted choked greetings over the hundred feet of still water that separated us. We hadn't seen each other since our last handshake in Australia, some 14,000 miles astern. More than once, I had doubted that we would be reunited here in Newport. Mark, perhaps better than any, could understand how hard, and how important, it had been for me to make it. I was glad that there were no boatloads of spectators around to disrupt this very private moment.

Vicki was not aboard *Lone Star*, which disappointed me momentarily until I realized that her decision to remain with the committee boat was the sensible one, the only way to guarantee that she would be able to step aboard *Joseph Young* the instant I crossed the finish line. Back below, I called Race Headquarters on the VHF radio, informing them of the present wind conditions and the resultant delay in my estimated time of arrival. Promising to inform them the minute the wind picked up, I settled in for a long wait.

For the next two hours I drifted, kept company by *Lone Star*, occasional puffs of wind ruffling our sails, moving us ever so slowly closer to the line. By noon, about the time I had expected to be sitting down to a full brunch ashore, *Joseph Young* and I were still a good four miles from the finish. As the minutes ticked away, a small but steady stream of tour boats and private craft began appearing from the mouth of the harbour. With my sails hanging slackly from the rigging, mocking my futile attempts to catch a little breeze, I began to get a little embarrassed. A few of the other competitors had come out on the tour boats to greet me, and jokes and sarcastic remarks on my sail-handling ability began to fly thick and fast.

The VHF radio suddenly came to life; a call from Robin Knox-Johnston on the Committee boat informed me that they were on their way out from the marina. On board were Vicki, my mother, brother, and friends from Nova Scotia. Heart in my mouth, I waited nervously, beside myself with impatience.

Within a few minutes the Committee boat hove into sight, drawing quickly closer until it lay stopped in the water a mere twenty feet from the side of *Joseph Young*. We had to stand, frustrated beyond reason, aching to hug and to hold, and able to do no more than gaze at one another, mouthing quiet hellos. I had not seen my mother, who had given me her whole-hearted support throughout the project, since last August. Vicki and I had last been together just after New Year in Sydney. As the Committee boat bearing my friends and family slowly drifted farther away, the waiting game began anew. This was certainly not the dashing finish that I had envisioned.

At long last a faint trace of wind began to drift across the water. It was now four o'clock in the afternoon, almost seven hours since I had first spotted Newport's bridge. As the sails filled, we began to move purposefully forward. Very soon now, it would be over. With the Committee boat standing by on the finish line, *Joseph Young* drew abeam of Brenton Reef Tower at 1643 hours local time to a fanfare of horns and whistles. Grinning from ear to ear, I experienced a feeling of satisfaction that surely cannot be equalled.

A little dazed, I moved forward to drop the jib for the last time. The Committee boat was racing towards me, prepared to take us in tow for the short trip into the marina. I had just stowed the jib and returned to the cockpit when it drew up alongside, and in a flash, Vicki was aboard and in my arms. We were all laughing and crying, hugs and handshakes were being shared across the rails. My brother David came aboard to lend a hand

and ended up doing all the work as the tow was connected and we set off for the marina. In the cockpit, champagne was cracked open; toasts were shared; the air was filled with incomparable feelings of joy and satisfaction.

Fifteen minutes later, we slipped around the end of the dock and into our allocated berth as "O Canada" was played over the loudspeakers. Amongst the crowds on the dock I could pick out some more of the other competitors and friends I had made in Newport during my time here ten months before. Inside, I was absolutely bursting with excitement, emotion, and relief at having completed the course. There was little time for reflection, however, as I was whisked away to the BOC office to answer questions from a host of reporters. Alone at sea, one's thoughts are only of the next day's weather, sail trim, or the next meal. World events shrink in importance, and now I found it overwhelming to be surrounded by so many people, all trying to feel a little of what my small personal world had been like. I was relieved when I was finally able to slip away and join Vicki, my mother, brother, and friends for a celebratory meal in the Goat Island pub. As food — that I hadn't had to cook — and drinks were brought to the table, and I looked about at my loved ones, it gradually began to sink in to me that it was over, it really was over. Months of fatigue and tension began to catch up to me, and soon Vicki and I slipped quietly away.

Three days later, the sixteen of us who had struggled around the world came together as a group for the last time at the prize-giving. The almost tangible, though unspoken, feeling of personal satisfaction and camaraderie that was present at the ceremony was, I knew, what I had not wanted to miss. Like anything worthwhile, this very personal victory had not come easily, but I knew I could never regret having paid the price. The pain, the hardship, and the fear would, with time, gradually be forgotten. This feeling of trials shared and challenges met could never fade.

For the next week Vicki and I enjoyed our first real holiday

173

together, making up for the months of separation. Good-byes were said frequently as family, friends, and the other competitors went their own ways. Life began slowly to return to normal.

At the end of the week I drove Vicki to Boston for her flight home, and then returned to Newport to make preparations for the sail back to Nova Scotia. For me, arriving at the Dartmouth Yacht Club would be the true finish of the voyage, for it was there that *Joseph Young* had first been launched, and from there that all the preparations, plans, and support had originated. The following day, quietly and with no fanfare, the lines were slipped for the very last time. Heading down Newport harbour for the open sea, *Joseph Young* was finally on her way home.

In Newport, I had been told emphatically by members of the support committee from the Dartmouth Yacht Club that I was to arrive off the mouth of Halifax harbour on the morning of June 14. Accordingly, I set out from Newport in plenty of time. Light winds were not uncommon at this time of the year so I allowed myself six days to cover the distance. Naturally, the winds were not light, and with a southerly gale blowing from astern as soon as we cleared the land, *Joseph Young* flew northward. It seemed almost as if she was as anxious to get home as I was. On June 12, a full forty-eight hours ahead of schedule, we crept forward in thin fog until the shoreline of Nova Scotia showed itself. Just around the corner lay Halifax harbour and home. It took great self-control to turn around and sail offshore again, but a promise was a promise, and so I settled down to wait out the next two days. In winds of over forty knots, we hove to under a triple-reefed mainsail for the night. The hours dragged by.

The following day I phoned the yacht club and gave them my position. A rendezvous was arranged for later that evening. Shortly after supper, visual contact was made with one of the club's power boats, and, after accepting a tow, we closed with the land once again to spend a rather strange last night at sea.

The morning of June 14 dawned wet and foggy, with the forecast providing no hope of any improvement. My luck with landfalls, it seemed, was still running true to form. As the appointed time drew near, we set off for the trip up the harbour, and into a true Nova Scotian welcome!

Not having been told what to expect, I was astounded at the reception I received. Literally hundreds of yachts and boats of all descriptions, all sounding their horns and whistles in a wild salute, emerged from the drizzle to take up stations astern, On either side of the harbour crowds of well-wishers had gathered to cheer and wave and celebrate my homecoming. I was filled with a real pride that I was able to call this place home. *Joseph Young* was led up the inner harbour and under the bridges. Slowly, the Dartmouth Yacht Club came into view, tucked away behind Navy Island. Under tow by a police boat now, we slid past the breakwater, and down the length of the marinas. Willing hands reached out to help as we glided in to the berth and the lines were made fast. Stepping ashore to a tumultuous welcome, I looked happily around me at the familiar surroundings. The voyage was truly over. *Joseph Young* and I had come home.

Epilogue

John and Vicki were married on September 2, 1988, in Halifax, Nova Scotia.

Following his return to Canada after the race, John has been giving numerous lectures about his voyage. Presently working for Search and Rescue with the Department of Transport, John is actively seeking sponsorship for the 1990/1991 BOC Challenge. He is keen to compete in a winning Class-One 60-foot racer, to be designed and built in Canada.

Joseph Young is presently up for sale.

Appendix

BOC CHALLENGE 1986-87
Leg Times and Total Elapsed Times By Class
(All times in days, hours, minutes, seconds: Placement in class)

Class I

Skipper Yacht	LOA	Leg I Time	(Place)	Leg II Time	(Place)	Leg III Time	(Place)	Leg IV Time	(Place)	Final Total	(Place)
Philippe Jeantot (FR) *Credit Agricole III*	60'	42:16:57:35	(2)	28:12:52:43	(2)	36:17:46:53	(1)	26:05:46:45	(3)	134:05:23:56	(1)
Titouan Lamazou (FR) *Ecureuil d'Aquitaine*	60'	46:08:04:22	(5)	28:07:13:22	(1)	36:21:15:45	(2)	26:05:02:37	(2)	137:17:36:06	(2)
Jean-Yves Terlain (FR) *UAP-Pour Médecins Sans Frontières*	60'	47:16:44:50	(6)	31:04:55:25	(3)	40:09:54:18	(3)	27:03:23:37	(7)	146:10:58:10	(3)
Guy Bernardin (USA) *Biscuits Lu*	59'10"	43:05:58:43	(3)	33:01:01:14	(5)	43:23:52:00	(4)	26:05:59:37	(4)	146:12:51:34	(4)
John Martin (SA) *Tuna Marine*	60'	42:01:10:36	(1)	35:04:16:20	(8)	44:01:56:44	(5)	26:00:50:20	(1)	147:08:14:00	(5)
Ian Kiernan (AUS) *Triple M/Spirit of Sydney*	59'11"	51:03:20:30	(8)	32:11:41:54	(4)	46:18:43:23	(7)	26:06:17:51	(5)	156:16:03:38	(6)
Bertie Reed (SA) *Stabilo Boss*	60'	50:17:39:48	(7)	40:18:09:43	(9)	45:23:10:31	(6)	26:10:42:54	(6)	163:21:42:56	(7)
David White (USA) *Legend Securities*	59'	51:17:20:20	(9)	34:14:23:25	(6)	51:08:56:20	(8)	27:06:25:17	(8)	164:23:05:22	(8)
Warren Luhrs (USA) *Thursday's Child*	60'	44:17:41:39	(4)	37:15:00:24	(8)	Retired before start of Leg III in Sydney after second dismasting					
Dick McBride (NZ) *Neptune's Express*	59'11"	Spent one month in Recife, Brazil, after Leg I dismasting; retired in Cape Town after completion of Leg I with mast problems									
John Biddlecombe (AUS) *ACI Crusader*	60'	Spent several weeks in Rio de Janeiro after injury from falling through hatch, and to affix bulb on keel; retired after accepting tow 62 miles from Leg I finish									

Class II

Skipper Yacht	LOA	Leg I Time	(Place)	Leg II Time	(Place)	Leg III Time	(Place)	Leg IV Time	(Place)	Final Total	(Place)
Mike Plant (USA) *Airco Distributor*	49'9"	47:15:30:30	(2)	34:16:03:52	(1)	47:03:00:00	(2)	28:01:10:22	(2)	157:11:44:44	(1)
Jean-Luc Van Den Heede (FR) *Let's Go*	45'	51:11:16:55	(3)	36:17:43:52	(3)	45:21:56:09	(1)	26:21:10:20	(1)	161:00:07:16	(2)
Harry Harkimo (FIN) *Belmont Finland*	50'	52:11:36:29	(5)	36:09:34:11	(2)	51:10:42:20	(4)	28:01:28:13	(3)	168:09:21:13	(3)
Hal Roth (USA) *American Flag*	50'	52:12:13:17	(6)	38:09:43:25	(5)	51:08:39:57	(3)	29:13:21:39	(4)	171:19:58:18	(4)
Richard Konkolski (USA) *Declaration of Independence*	44'	51:11:34:15	(4)	38:10:42:00	(6)	51:11:25:58	(5)	30:20:58:50	(7)	172:06:41:03	(5)
Mark Schrader (USA) *Lone Star*	47'	54:10:59:30	(8)	38:09:02:20	(4)	52:08:42:24	(6)	30:09:39:38	(6)	175:14:23:52	(6)
Pentti Salmi (FIN) *Colt By Rettig*	44'	53:18:55:22	(7)	39:18:27:32	(7)	52:09:28:46	(7)	29:19:10:59	(5)	175:18:02:39	(7)
John Hughes (CAN) *Joseph Young*	41'2"	55:00:23:52	(9)	39:23:49:40	(9)	92:11:27:38	(8)	37:02:14:14	(8)	224:13:55:24	(8)
Harry Mitchell (GB) *Double Cross*	40'9"	66:07:46:31	(10)	55:03:56:21	(9)	Retired in New Zealand at beginning of Leg III after running aground					
Jacques de Roux (FR) *Skoiern IV*	50'	45:14:47:10	(1)	Lost overboard 250 miles from completion of Leg II in Sydney							
Dick Cross (USA) *Airforce*	44'5"	Boat lost at sea approx. 130 miles north-east of Bermuda after Leg I collision with unidentified object; skipper rescued by Navy chopper									
Mac Smith (USA) *Quailo*	44'4"	Retired in Rio de Janeiro after suffering rig problems in knockdown during Leg I									
Takao Shimada (JAP) *Madonna*	48'	Retired in Rio de Janeiro with rigging problems during Leg I									
Eduardo de Almeida (BR) *Miss Global*	40'5"	Retired in Brazil after second rudder failure during Leg I									

Times above include all penalties and adjustments.

Reprinted with permission of *Cruising World*

179

Glossary

Italicized words in the definitions are also defined in the glossary.

Aft at, near, or towards the back, or stern, of the boat.

Argos beacon installed on all the yachts by the Race Committee, these beacons automatically transmitted the position, course, and speed of each boat to Race Headquarters at least once every twenty-four hours. The information was read by a satellite passing overhead and relayed via a receiving station in France. The beacons did not provide any information directly to the competitors.

Auto-pilot an electrically powered self-steering device that keeps the boat on a set compass course.

Baby-stay a *stay* that runs from a point part-way up the mast *forward* to a *chainplate* located on the centre-line of the boat between the mast and the bow.

Backstay the stay that runs from the top of the mast back to the stern of the boat.

Beam-ends a term originating from the time when sailing ships were built of wood, and had deck beams running from one side of the ship to the other. The ends of these beams fitted against the sides of the hull. Thus, when a vessel is ''thrown on her beam ends,'' she is knocked down onto her side by the wind or waves.

Block a nautical term for a pulley.

Boom the spar to which the bottom edge, or foot, of the *mainsail* is fastened. The *forward* end of the boom is attached to the mast.

Boom vang a series of *blocks* and rope running from the underside of the *boom* to a point on the mast at deck level. It prevents the boom from lifting with the force of the wind in the *mainsail*.

Bow pulpit the steel railing that is fitted around the bow of the boat.

Broad-reach the point of sail where the wind is blowing from a direction over the *quarter*. It is generally the fastest point of sail.

Bulkhead a structural ''wall'' inside the boat, running from one side of the boat to the other.

Burgee a private flag showing the colours of a yacht club or other organization.

Cabin sole the floor.

Chainplate steel plate fastened to the hull or deck to which the lower ends of the *shrouds* and *stays* are attached.

Checkstay a stay that runs from a point part-way up the mast back to the stern.

Cockpit the sunken area of the deck where one can sit down and steer the boat.

Companionway the entranceway from the deck into the cabin.

Dead reckoning the process of estimating the boat's position based on the course steered, the speed, and the elapsed time since the last position fix.

Electronic log an electronic device for measuring the speed of the boat through the water. A small paddle-wheel protruding from the bottom of the boat sends an electrical signal to the display unit.

Forepeak *forward* storage compartment in the boat.

Forestay stay that runs from near the top of the mast *forward* to the bow of the boat where it is attached to the *chainplate* on the *stemhead*.

Forward towards the front or bow of the boat.

Foul-weather gear yachtsman's oilskins or rain clothes.

Genoa a sail hoisted on the forestay, numbered according to the size —a #1 is large, for light winds; a #4 is smaller, for strong winds.

Gybe a manoeuvre where the boat's course is altered to bring the wind from one side of the boat to the other by swinging the stern through the eye of the wind.

Halyard the line that is secured to the top of the sail and is used to raise or lower it.

Hank a metal clip permanently fastened to the front or leading edge of the *jib* or *Genoa*. The hanks are used to attach the sail to the *forestay*.

Head nautical term for a toilet.

Headsail general term for a sail hoisted and flown forward of the mast.

Hove-to   a yacht is hove-to when she is sitting with the bow pointing into the wind and waves, and the sails trimmed so that the speed is almost nil. It is a tactic used by some sailors to ride out a storm.

Jackstay   a wire attached to the deck at the bow and stern and running the length of the boat. When one is working on deck, a short line from one's safety harness can be clipped onto the jackstay as a safety precaution.

Jib   a sail hoisted on the *forestay*, slightly different in shape to a *Genoa*.

Keel   the fin-like appendage on the bottom of the hull. On a sailboat the keel is normally made of lead and is needed to balance the force of the wind on the sails and so keep the boat upright.

Knot   a unit measure of a boat's speed; one knot equals one nautical mile per hour.

Leeward   on the side away from the wind, or the direction towards which the wind is blowing.

Log   device for measuring the speed of the boat through the water.

Log-book   the official document containing an account of the voyage.

Log impeller   the small paddle-wheel or propeller, part of the *log*, which protrudes below the hull and is turned by the water when the boat is in motion.

Mainsail   as the name implies, the main sail, hoisted on the *aft* side of the mast.

Nautical mile   the mile used for navigation at sea; it is equal to 1.15 statute miles.

Port   the left-hand side of the boat when facing towards the bow.

Port tack   a yacht is on the port tack when the wind is blowing from a direction that lies off the boat's *port* side.

Quarter   the part of the boat's side near the stern. Also refers to the wind or waves coming from that direction; e.g., a quartering sea.

Reach   the number of miles sailed on one *tack*. Also used to define a point of sail, such as a *broad reach*.

Reef   that section of the *mainsail* that can be folded down and then tied along the *boom*—once the sail is partially lowered—to reduce the sail area as the wind increases in strength. There are generally a number of reefs on the sail, which are successively taken in as necessary. To let a reef out as the wind decreases in strength is to "shake out a reef."

Rhumb line   in navigation this is a straight line between two points on a normal chart. Due to the curvature of the earth, however, it is not actually the shortest distance between the two points.

Running backstay   a *stay* between a point part-way up the mast and the back of the boat. It is attached to the mast below the *backstay* and above the *checkstay*.

Runner   an abbreviation for *running backstay*.

Running rigging   the ropes and wires that are used to control, hoist, and adjust the sails.

Safety harness   a harness that is worn when there is a danger of falling overboard; it has a line attached to it that can be clipped on to the *jackstay* or other point on the boat.

Satellite navigator   an electronic navigational aid that uses signals received from satellites to determine the boat's position.

Self-steering   a general term for the *auto-pilot* and the *windvane*.

Shackle   normally a U-shaped metal fitting with a screw-in pin between the open ends of the U, used to fasten one thing to another.

Shroud   a wire that supports the mast, connected from the mast to a *chainplate* at the side of the hull.

Sheet   a rope attached to the corner of a sail used to control the angle at which the sail is set. A jib sheet controls the *jib*, the main sheet the *mainsail*, etc.

Single-sideband radio   a standard type of ship-to-ship and ship-to-shore radio used for communicating by voice over distances of up to several thousand miles.

Slatting   slapping, striking, or beating.

Spinnaker pole   a pole used as a temporary spar to hold out the bottom corner of the spinnaker, a large sail used when sailing downwind. When in use, one end of the pole clips onto the mast, the other end supports the sail. On *Joseph Young* I carried two spinnaker poles, each about eighteen feet long.

Spreaders   horizontal bars extending from either side of the mast, like crosstrees. The *shrouds* pass over the tips of the spreaders.

Stanchion   vertical post that supports the lifelines or railing around the edge of the deck.

Standing rigging   the wires, *shrouds*, and *stays* that support the mast.

Stay   a wire that supports the mast in the *forward* and *aft* direction.

Stemhead   the very front of the boat on the deck level.

Strop   a lashing of rope with a loop left free, a strap.

Survival pack   a container holding the various items of survival equipment carried by the yachts in the race for use in a liferaft.

Transom   the flat part of the hull at the very back of the boat.

Traveller   a device used to control the *mainsail sheet*. The traveller consists of a car that slides on a track from one side of the boat to the other. One end of the main sheet is attached to this car, the other end to the *boom*.

Trisail   a small, strongly made sail that is hoisted in place of the *mainsail* when the wind reaches storm force. On *Joseph Young*, this bright orange sail served as a mainsail on the jury-rig.

Weather rail   a rail runs around the edge of the deck on most yachts. That part of the rail, or side of the yacht, that is facing the oncoming wind and waves is called the weather rail.

Windvane   a mechanical self-steering device, mounted on the *transom*, which automatically steers the boat, keeping the wind at a constant angle relative to the wind direction.

Windward   towards the wind. The windward side of the boat is that side facing the direction from which the wind is blowing. If another boat or object is sighted ''to windward,'' it can be seen by looking in the direction from which the wind is blowing. The opposite of *leeward*.

Acknowledgements

Throughout my circumnavigation there were many people who gave freely and unselfishly of their time to make it possible for me to realize my goal. Some of the names I never knew; some, sadly, I may have forgotten, though never can I forget their faces, their actions, or their kind thoughts. To any whose names may not appear here I offer my apologies and, of course, my thanks.

To the following people, my unofficial support team, I can only say thank you — the difficult jobs they handled instantly, the impossible took just a little longer: John Sandford, Susan and John Mellamby, Ron and Christine Hurst, Jim MacDonald, all the members of the Dartmouth Yacht Club and the support committee; Stephen Murch; Colin Smith; Judy O'Brien; Joan Harbinson; Nina and Norman Maclennan; Wayne, Brian, Bev, and Tracey Hunter; the members of the British forces on the Falkland Islands; Robin Knox-Johnston and the other BOC competitors; amateur radio operators worldwide; Robin Davie; and special love and thanks to Victoria and my family, who endured for so long. Particular appreciation goes to National Sea Products Limited for their timely and generous support. Thanks also to the people of Dartmouth, Halifax, Nova Scotia, and Canada. And finally, thanks to Joseph Young, my grandfather, who knew.

Edited by Sarah Reid
Designed by David Shaw & Associates Ltd.
Composition by
Compeer Typographic Services Limited
Manufactured by
D. W. Friesen